INDIGENOUS FILMS

Series Editors

Randolph Lewis
David Delgado Shorter

The Fast Runner: Filming the Legend of Atanarjuat

MICHAEL ROBERT EVANS

UNIVERSITY OF NEBRASKA PRESS | LINCOLN AND LONDON

Publication of this volume was
assisted by The Virginia Faulkner
Fund, established in memory of
Virginia Faulker, editor in chief of
the University of Nebraska Press.

Photos by author.

Library of Congress Cataloging-in-
Publication Data

Evans, Michael Robert, 1959–
The fast runner : filming the legend of
Atanarjuat / Michael Robert Evans.
p. cm. — (Indigenous films)
Includes bibliographical references and
index.
ISBN 978-0-8032-2208-3 (pbk. : alk.
paper)
1. Atanarjuat (Motion picture) I. Title.
PN1997.2.A73E93 2010
791.43'72 — dc22
2009039685

Set in Minion by Kim Essman.
Designed by Nathan Putens.

To Joanna, Dylan,

and Miles Evans,

my inspirational family,

and to Henry Glassie,

my inspirational mentor

CONTENTS

ILLUSTRATIONS

ACKNOWLEDGMENTS

Zacharias Kunuk, Norman Cohn, Pauloosie Qulitalik, Pacome Qulaut, and other Isuma producers helped me in personal and professional ways as I gathered the information presented in this book. I am grateful for their patience and assistance.

Other people in Igloolik were extraordinarily helpful as well, especially John and Carolyn MacDonald, Leah Otak, Julie Ivalu, and Jake Kadluk. My experience and my understanding were enhanced by all of you.

NOTE

I have previously published a book about Igloolik Isuma Productions, titled *Isuma: Inuit Video Art*. That book, published by McGill–Queens University Press, includes a chapter on *The Fast Runner*. It also contains material about the people of Isuma and other facets important to this story. While the writing for this book is original, some of the information is necessarily similar to the information in *Isuma: Inuit Video Art*.

Also, *The Fast Runner* was shot in digital format and then converted to film for distribution. It was then released again in digital formats, including DVD, for home viewing. So, despite the distinct and significant differences between film and video technologies, in what follows I refer to *The Fast Runner* and other Isuma products as "films," "movies," or "videos" fairly interchangeably.

Finally, I should point out that the English-alphabet spelling of Inuit words and names varies widely. When quoting material from printed sources, I have kept the spelling used by those sources, even when that spelling varies from other uses elsewhere in the book.

Randolph Lewis, David Delgado Shorter

We are proud to have Michael Evans's *"The Fast Runner": Filming the Legend of Atanarjuat* as the first entry in the new book series, Indigenous Films. For the past three years we have sought out scholars we consider uniquely qualified to write about a particular film as a portal to the Native culture it depicts. The series will feature concise books on individual Native films, including *The Fast Runner, Whale Rider, Dances with Wolves, Black Robe, Smoke Signals, Apocalypto, Little Big Man, Navajo Talking Picture, Pocahontas,* and other films made by or about indigenous people. Each book in the series will provide an affordable and accessible companion to an important film that is often taught in history, anthropology, folklore, or Native American studies but for which there are few existing supporting materials or companion pieces to help instructors and students access the key issues in the film. We want each book to be written in an accessible manner and to examine the film from a number of angles that should stimulate classroom discussion, but also to engage a larger critical conversation about the power and potential of indigenous media. Our ultimate goal is to challenge the Eurocentrism that often afflicts the study of cinema, and to initiate conversations about the promises and challenges of indigenous media now emerging around the globe.

The Fast Runner is an ideal place to begin. Along with *Smoke Signals, The Fast Runner* remains one of the key texts in the burgeoning field of indigenous media. We believe that this extraordinary film represents a breakthrough in terms of autonomous production, aesthetic ambition, and critical reception. How many films have received rave reviews from Margaret Atwood ("like Homer with a video camera"), Claude Lévi-Strauss, Jacques Chirac, and Roger Ebert? *The Fast Runner* is unusual in attracting the attention of novelists, scholars, politicians, and general film audiences, all of whom seem to view it as a watershed moment in the history of indigenous filmmaking, not simply for Inuit people but for Native film in the broadest sense. Almost every major reviewer fawned over it and what it seemingly represents: an epic film that artfully married the latest in video technology with the traditional storytelling of the Inuit. Reading Michael Evans's book confirmed our sense that *The Fast Runner* is one of the most significant films yet produced by indigenous filmmakers.

Beyond its role as a touchstone for Native film, *The Fast Runner* also has great significance to Canadian media: it led Canadian films at the box office in 2002, and has since been selected as one of the top ten Canadian films of all time. Clearly, a great deal can be said about this film. The relationship between *The Fast Runner* and its represented subject, Inuit culture, is worthy of much discussion across a wide range of academic disciplines, including Canadian studies, visual anthropology, ethnohistory, film studies, indigenous studies, and religious studies.

We encouraged Michael Evans to write this book after reading his earlier work on indigenous media. We believed he was ideally positioned to do so: almost no one else has the ethnographic experience with Inuit media that he has acquired (he lived there for the better part of a year, working with the Inuit Broadcasting Corporation). Almost no one else has thought about Inuit media and their role in Inuit culture in the folkloric way that he has. Based on extensive research and personal connections in the Arctic, as well as a wealth of cultural knowledge and considerable sensitivity, his book is a uniquely well-informed, thoughtful, and illuminating look at Inuit creativity in the age of electronic media. Evans shows how *The Fast Runner*'s producers, Zacharias Kunuk and Norman Cohn, handled their complex intercultural collaboration with extraordinary skill, resulting in a film that can serve as a model of autonomous media production for indigenous people.

One of our goals for this series was to encourage teachers to use more Native film in the classroom. With its short chapters and clear prose style, Michael Evans's book strikes an appropriate balance between scholarly depth and narrative flow, making it both teachable in the undergraduate classroom and readable by the nonspecialist.

Anyone interested in the intricacies of a great story—and the legend of Atanarjuat certainly qualifies—will enjoy this book.

As editors of the Indigenous Films book series, we are proud to have this work as the starting point in what we hope will be a long and fruitful conversation about the beauty and power of indigenous media.

Follow the western shore of Hudson Bay northward until the wide expanse of water crimps into a sliver of the Arctic Ocean called the Fury and Hecla Strait. The island looming to the north and east—the fifth-largest island in the world—is Baffin Island, home to caribou herds and Inuit villages and Iqaluit, the capital of the new Canadian territory of Nunavut. Tucked between Baffin Island and the mainland is a much smaller island, shaped like a cracked stone. This is Igloolik Island, and hugging one side of the bay that nearly splits it is the Inuit community of Igloolik, "place of houses."

From the village, a short ride by all-terrain vehicle around the hook of Turton Bay brings you to a stone—rectangular, reddish brown, covered with bird droppings. This stone offers a pleasant place to sit and gaze across the expanse of rocky beach toward the small waves of the sheltered bay. It was on this rock that a young man named Atanarjuat sat, centuries ago, to wait for the whales he had hunted to drift up on shore.

According to a legend still told in the Arctic, Atanarjuat and his brother were attacked one day by rivals who were jealous of their skill and popularity. The rivals knocked down the brothers' tent and stabbed their spears through the fabric, killing the brother. Atanarjuat managed to escape, however, and he fled—totally naked—across the frozen ocean. The rivals pursued him, intent on murder. But Atanarjuat was endowed with extraordinary foot speed and was able to stay ahead of them, even though the cold sapped his strength and the ice slashed his feet. Ultimately, Atanarjuat escaped his pursuers and was nursed back to health by a family on a distant island. Once he was strong enough, he returned to Igloolik and exacted revenge on his rivals.

Legends such as this one infuse Inuit culture with interpretations of events, lessons about morality and social responsibility, and ideas about how to live and thrive in the Arctic. But most of the world knows about the Inuit not through their legends and stories but through southern depictions of life in the North — portrayals that often position the Inuit not as wise and resourceful but as savage and primitive. Or backward and unable to adapt to the changing world. Or silly and happy-go-lucky. Or irrelevant and essentially nonexistent. In the face of these depictions in literature and film, increasing numbers of Inuit artists are offering counterpoints that show the richness, depth, and genius inherent in Inuit culture. One such group is Igloolik Isuma Productions, and its most influential film so far is based on the Atanarjuat legend.

Released in 2001, *The Fast Runner* is the first feature-length film written, directed, and produced by Inuit moviemakers, and one of the most important indigenous films ever made.[1] It has had a profound impact in several spheres: Inuit moviemaking, life in Igloolik, the understanding and appreciation of Inuit life and perspectives worldwide.

The Fast Runner represents a significant leap for Isuma, but it rests on a solid body of previous work. The group and its primary producer, Zacharias Kunuk, began with short pieces about traditional Inuit life and perspectives; some of the early pieces were scripted, but others were done in a more documentary style. After an initial string of interesting and innovative videos, the organization focused on the creation of the Nunavut series, thirteen videos showing Inuit approaches to dogsledding, seal hunting, and other activities. Isuma produced a few more videos, taking various approaches to issues involving life in the North, while arranging the funding for their ambitious *Fast Runner* project.

The success of *The Fast Runner* contributed to the reputation of Igloolik in the realm of Inuit videography. Three video groups are active in the community: Igloolik Isuma Productions, the Tariagsuk Video Centre (a community video organization), and a cultural-programming branch of the Inuit Broadcasting Corporation. All three groups have been creating movies for more than two decades, but the international success of *The Fast Runner* brought newfound attention and respect to Isuma's work in particular and Inuit videography in general.

The core of Isuma comprises two men: Zacharias Kunuk and Norman Cohn. Kunuk has lived in the Igloolik area his whole life, and in addition to producing videos he is also a skilled carver and storyteller. Born in an outpost camp on the edge of the Arctic Ocean, he was taken from his family while still a boy and enrolled in a boarding school. He was eventually reunited with his family, which moved into permanent settlement in the village of Igloolik. Kunuk's first language is Inuktitut, although he speaks fluent English with a deliberate pace and distinctive accent. He lives with his wife and children in a simple house on the western side of town.

Cohn is not Inuit. He is a Caucasian video artist from southern Canada, and he met Kunuk when he led a video training session sponsored by the Inuit Broadcasting Corporation. He splits his time between Igloolik and Montreal, where Isuma has an increasingly strong presence. His role as the only non-Inuk in the Isuma organization raises interesting questions about identity and perspective that I discuss later in this book.

For decades, the world has been aware of the grace and power of Inuit sculpture and printmaking; with the global success of *The Fast Runner*, people are awakening to the artistry, the depth, and the perspectives of Inuit films. *The Fast Runner* has been shown in dozens of countries, earning awards at a host of film and video festivals. Perhaps the most prestigious is the Camera d'Or Award, presented to Kunuk at the 2001 Cannes Film Festival; the award is given to the best work by a new director. Other international awards garnered by *The Fast Runner* include the Guardian Award for Best New Director (co-winner) at the Edinburgh International Film Festival, the Grand Prix of the Flemish Community Award for Best Film at the Flanders International Film Festival, and the Best Feature Film Award at both the Santa Fe International Festival and the San Diego International Film Festival.

The movie has earned numerous Canadian awards as well, including the Best Canadian Feature Film Award at the Toronto International Film Festival, the Special Jury Prize and the Prix du Public at the Festival International du Nouveau Cinema et des Nouveaux

Medias de Montreal, and five Genie Awards (the Canadian equivalent of the Oscars), for Best Picture, Best Director, Best Screenplay, Best Original Score, and Best Editing. For many of these awards, including the Cannes and Genie awards, Kunuk gave his acceptance speech in Inuktitut, the language of the Inuit and the language of the film.

The Fast Runner received praise from prominent reviewers, including A. O. Scott in the *New York Times*, Jim Hoberman in the *Village Voice*, Margaret Atwood in the *Globe and Mail*, and Roger Ebert in the *Chicago Sun-Times*, among many others. Jacques Chirac, then president of France, added his praise for the film as well.

And the admiration for *The Fast Runner* goes beyond the popular and the political. Anthropologist Claude Lévi-Strauss wrote that the film offers

> superb landscapes, admirably photographed, which, for long moments, carry the spectator off to this "other world." . . . I was also captivated by many ethnographic details and by the human realness of the characters. It is exciting to see Inuit people reconstitute themselves from an emotionally moving legend — the framework of their traditional life, the daily tasks, and the life events. (Igloolik Isuma Productions, 2002, 9)

The Fast Runner is a complex movie — watching the three-hour film in which nothing but Inuktitut is spoken requires active engagement by the audience — and its role in Inuit life and the presentation of Inuit culture to the world is far-reaching and profound. Producer Zacharias Kunuk put it this way:

> Atanarjuat wasn't the only legend we heard but it was one of the best — once you get that picture into your head of that naked man running for his life across the ice, his hair flying, you never forget it. It had everything in it for a fantastic movie — love, jealousy, murder and revenge, and at the same time, buried in this ancient Inuit "action thriller," were all these lessons we kids were supposed to learn about how if you break these taboos that

kept our ancestors alive, you could be out there running for *your* life just like him! (Igloolik Isuma Productions, 2002, 13)

I was drawn to the Arctic out of a love for Inuit art and culture, including videos and film. I spent nine months with Isuma, during the creation of *The Fast Runner*, and myriad hours talking with Kunuk and the other producers and viewing Isuma's body of videos. Ultimately, I wrote my doctoral dissertation on the work of Isuma and the other video organizations in Igloolik, and I now teach journalism at Indiana University and focus my research on indigenous media. In particular, I explore how indigenous artists express their culture through the externally developed media of newspapers, magazines, radio and television programs, and videos.

In this book, I offer some keys to help unlock the multiple facets of this intricate and historic movie. I describe the plot, which can be hard to follow at times, and I set the film in its cultural, social and historical contexts. I also explain some of the choices made by the producers, including their decision to change the usual ending of the legend to create a more pointed conclusion to the film. The goal of this book is a deeper and clearer understanding of — and appreciation for — this groundbreaking film.

ATANARJUAT'S FAMILY

Tulimaq, father of Atanarjuat and Aamarjuaq.

Pitaaluk, Tulimaq's wife and mother of Atanarjuat and Aamarjuaq.

Aamarjuaq, son of Tulimaq and Pitaaluk and Atanarjuat's older brother.

Atanarjuat, the central figure of the film and legend.

Kumaglak, son of Atanarjuat and Atuat.

UQI'S FAMILY

Kumaglak, the camp leader at the start of the film. A powerful shaman.

Panikpak, Kumaglak's wife. Also a shaman.

Sauri, son of Kumaglak and Panikpak. He ushers in the evil shaman that disrupts the camp's harmony.

Kukilasak, Sauri's wife.

Uqi, son of Sauri and Kukilasak. He murders his father to become camp leader.

Puja, daughter of Sauri and Kukilasak (hence Uqi's sister). She seduces Atanarjut, becomes his wife, then betrays him.

The characters in *The Fast Runner* are numerous and sometimes difficult to keep straight. One particular challenge in the film is that the beloved camp leader Kumaglak was the father of the evil Sauri, so that family went from "good" to "bad" in the course of one generation. This chart organizes the characters by family and lists them by generation. The main characters are listed in boldface.

QULITALIK'S FAMILY	ATUAT'S FAMILY	OTHERS
Qulitalik, older brother of Panikpak. A powerful shaman.	Utuqiaq, Atuat's father.	Tuurngarjuaq, an evil shaman. Invited into the camp by Sauri, he brings trouble with him.
Niriuniq, Qulitalik's wife.	Sakku, Atuat's mother.	Asa, Ulluriaq's mother.
Kigutikarjuk, adopted daughter of Qulitalik and Niriuniq.	**Atuat**, daughter of Utuqiaq and Sakku. Promised to Uqi as a child, she falls in love with Atanarjuat.	Sigluk, Ulluriaq's father
		Ulluriaq, Aamarjuaq's wife.
		Pakak, one of Uqi's sidekicks.
		Pittiulaq, one of Uqi's sidekicks.
		Qillaq, father of Uqi's and Pittiulak's wives.

PRONUNCIATION OF NAMES

Aamarjuaq	ah-MAR-joo-ahk
Asa	AH-sah
Atanarjuat	ah-tah-NAR-joo-aht
Atuat	AH-tuat
Kigutikarjuk	kee-goo-tee-KAR-jook
Kukilasak	koo-KEE-luh-sock
Kumaglak	koo-MUG-luck
Niriuniq	nee-ree-YOO-nirk
Pakak	PAH-kahk
Panikpak	PAH-nick-pahk
Pitaaluk	pee-TAH-look
Pittiulaq	pit-tee-YOO-lahk
Puja	POO-yah
Qulitalik	khoo-LIT-tah-lick
Qillaq	KHEED-lahk
Sakku	SOCK-koo
Sauri	SAOW-ree
Sigluk	SEEG-look
Tulimaq	too-lee-MAHK
Tuurngarjuaq	toong-GAHR-joo-ahk
Ulluriaq	oo-DLOO-ree-yahk
Uqi	oo-khee
Utuqiaq	oo-TOO-khee-yahk

THE FAST RUNNER

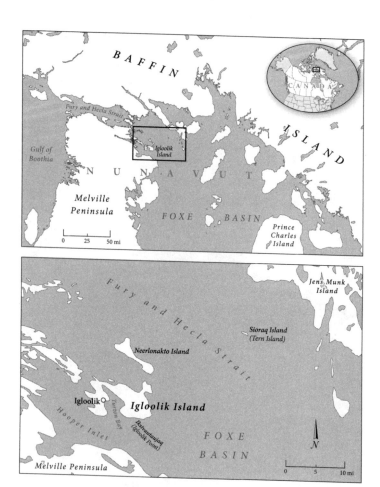

Igloolik, which is both the setting for *The Fast Runner* and Isuma's base of operations, is a small island between mainland Canada and Baffin Island. The hamlet of Igloolik occupies one side of Turton Bay, which cuts deeply into Igloolik Island. Sioraq, the island to which Atanarjuat ran while being chased by his attackers, lies a short distance to the east.

CHAPTER ONE

The Context of the Creation

Any expression of culture loses meaning when separated from its context. Without an understanding of the circumstances in which the art was created — the physical, social, and spiritual environments within which the creation happened — the significance of the work and the lessons it offers dwindle into impotence. Through *The Fast Runner* and other videos, Igloolik Isuma Productions spans two major contexts: the world depicted in the films and the world of today, in which Isuma goes about its work and shows its films to audiences. Linking these contexts is a stream of history half a century long.

When Zacharias Kunuk and others at Isuma created *The Fast Runner*, one of their goals was to show audiences the resiliency of Inuit and the ingenuity with which they have long faced the physical and social challenges of life in the Arctic. The producers wanted to help audiences appreciate that while conditions were sometimes harsh, Inuit nevertheless created a world filled with laughter, jealousy, hope, hatred, faith, fear, and all the other attributes that make life everywhere complex and intricate.

But in speeches and in some of his videos, Kunuk also emphasizes the modern side of the Arctic, pointing out that while some facets of Inuit life have remained unchanged since Atanarjuat's time, others have evolved dramatically. This evolution does not, he insists, fall into the standard two stereotypical camps. One stereotype positions the Inuit as soulless victims of modernity, forced to forge ahead without the solace and support of the long-standing heritage and traditions that have been stripped from them. The other positions Inuit as bewildered, intimidated anachronisms, clinging desperately to their past and lacking any hope for the future. Both views advance the racist ideas, still tragically prevalent in modern Canada, that

Inuit are adrift, ill-suited to the demands of the working world, and prone to alcoholism.

Kunuk and the other Isuma producers offer a third view, one that shows the Inuit in a more realistic light. In this view, Inuit embrace the more useful opportunities and improvements that the modern world offers while at the same time holding on to the traditions, beliefs, and attitudes that continue to serve them well. Inuit do not blindly clutch the old ways, afraid to discard any of their past. Like all rational people, they keep what works. And they neither fear nor misunderstand the present; instead, they adopt practices that offer significant benefits and meld them with older approaches that are still worth keeping. The modern Arctic is not a baffling place for the Inuit, nor is it alien and cut off from all that came before. The changes in the North have been rapid and sometimes devastating, but Inuit live in the modern world just as fully as everyone else.

Geographically, the island of Igloolik has changed little since Atanarjuat fled its shores. The highest point on the island is the ridge that runs to the northeast of the town's current location. Today, the Igloolik cemetery is on the ridge. In Inuit fashion, reflecting not only tradition but also practicality, many of the graves still consist of stone walls and a thick layer of loose stones placed over the body. The ridge is not very high and is quite easy to climb; overall, the Igloolik area is extraordinarily flat. Melville Peninsula — the Canadian mainland — can be seen off in the distance to the south.

As it has been for millennia, almost all of the island is covered with rock and tundra. The tundra, which can be found in the interior of the island, is spongy and wet in the summer and can make for difficult walking. It is sometimes deep and can suck a hiker's boots off; Atanarjuat is fortunate that his pursuers did not chase him inland in the early summer. The beaches on all sides of the island consist of loose stone, most often limestone and granite, offering wonderful opportunities for finding fossils.

There is one significant geographic and geologic change since Atanarajuat's time: the island is slowly rising. When glaciers covered the region during the last ice age, they compressed the ground below them. Once they receded, the land began to spring back slowly, freed from the massive weight of ice and snow. The rock where Atanarjuat sat to wait for his whales to drift ashore is now about five hundred feet back from the waterline.

History

According to archaeological evidence, Igloolik was first occupied by humans approximately four thousand years ago.[1] The earliest people are believed to be those belonging to the Dorset culture, the name archaeologists give to the people who occupied the eastern Canadian Arctic for nearly fifteen hundred years. Inuit continue to tell stories about the Tuniit, giant people who lived in the area long ago. It is possible that the tales are describing the Dorset people who were in the eastern Arctic when the modern-day Inuit arrived in the region.

Throughout the centuries that Inuit have lived in the Arctic, migrating in spurts from west to east, shamanism has been the dominant spiritual practice. This span was broken only by the adoption of Christianity in recent decades, a theme addressed by several Isuma movies, including *The Journals of Knud Rasmussen*. In *The Fast Runner*, set in a time before the arrival of Europeans, shamanism plays a potent role in influencing the actions and attitudes of the human characters.

One major feature of Igloolik's oral history refers to the migration of a group of Inuit from the Igloolik area and farther west. The group was led by a shaman named Qillaq, who decided to travel eastward in the mid-nineteenth century — about four hundred years after the Atanarjuat saga took place — to avoid a vicious feud with another shaman that threatened the lives of his followers and himself. With about forty others, including some from the Igloolik area, he migrated to Greenland to start a new camp and a new life. When he arrived in northwest Greenland, his followers considered his leadership so exemplary that they renamed him "the Great Qillaq." The Greenlandic form of his name is spelled Qitdlaq, and "the Great Qitdlaq" is Qitdlarssuaq, which is how he is known to this day. Many people in Igloolik are related to members of this band of travelers.

As *The Fast Runner* makes clear, the Igloolik area was well occupied by the time the first Europeans arrived. The first European ships to reach Igloolik were the *Fury* and the *Hecla*, which arrived in the area in 1822; the Fury and Hecla Strait, which separates Igloolik from mainland Canada, was named after these vessels. The expedition was commanded by Captain William Edward Parry, who was searching for the Northwest Passage. Parry failed in his mission, but he learned a great deal about the Arctic and Inuit. Two Inuit who befriended him, Iligliuk and Ewerat, drew detailed maps showing the intricate coastline of the region. But stories in the Igloolik region mention that Parry's voyage was cursed by a powerful shaman, who drove Parry back to Europe and banned all other Europeans from coming to the area. Decades passed before any other Europeans made it to Igloolik.

The Igloolik region probably was visited by the Franklin expedition in the mid-nineteenth century. John Franklin was the commander of *Erebus* and the *Terror*, and he was determined to be the one who found the Northwest Passage. He made it beyond Igloolik, but then his ships and crew vanished. Traces that have been found since show that the expedition got as far west as King William Island before the ships were crushed in the ice and abandoned. Franklin and his surviving men set off on foot in an effort to reach a village to the south, but they never made it. Scurvy, discipline problems, and lead poisoning from the cans that held their food rations contributed to the disaster, as did the British habit at the time of adhering to their own customs and approaches without regard to the technologies that allowed the Inuit to thrive in the Arctic. The British sailors wore cotton and wool, lived in canvas tents, and ate food they had brought from home. The Inuit, as *The Fast Runner* shows, wore much more appropriate clothing made of caribou, wolf, bear, and seal, lived in igloos and sod houses, and ate the animals they hunted. In this way the Inuit were warm and healthy, gaining all the vitamins, nourishment, and calories they needed from the animals' meat and fat. Scurvy, the result of a vitamin C deficiency, was nonexistent among the Inuit, but it cursed numerous British expeditions. Frostbite, hypothermia, and other hazards of the North also contributed to the demise of the Franklin expedition, all within sight of Inuit who were living well in the same area.

An American named Charles Francis Hall became convinced that he could find some survivors of the Franklin expedition, and he ventured to the Igloolik area in 1867 and 1868. He failed to find any Franklin sailors, but he contributed to southern knowledge of the Inuit. In particular, he enthusiastically embraced the Inuit way of life in the North. He lived in igloos, wore caribou clothing, and adopted the Inuit diet. His success at living in the "inhospitable" North — and having a good time while he was at it — encouraged subsequent explorers to pay closer attention to the wisdom gained by the Inuit over four millennia of Arctic living.

Perhaps the most significant early visit by Europeans to the Igloolik area came in 1921, when Knud Rasmussen arrived. Rasmussen was a Greenlander who was half Inuit, and he spoke Inuktitut well. He organized and led an expedition to Arctic North America to learn more about the people and the geography there. He spent considerable time in the Igloolik region, learning from the Inuit and recording a wide range of information: language, social customs, natural history, geology, and more.

Rasmussen's arrival in Igloolik is the subject of Isuma's second major feature film. Titled *The Journals of Knud Rasmussen*, it chronicles the meeting from the Inuit point of view. Characters in the film express their concerns that this new arrival might threaten their traditions and devalue their knowledge and wisdom. Where *The Fast Runner* shows Inuit life from five hundred years ago, *Journals* shows the moment at which that life began its sharp shift, with the first arrival of Europeans on the island of Igloolik. *Journals* positions *The Fast Runner* as something of a baseline against which the changes foreshadowed in *Journals* take on greater significance.

In the 1930s, not long after Rasmussen's visits, the Roman Catholic Church established a permanent mission just outside Igloolik, in a place called Avaja. It was the first permanent occupation of the area by non-Inuit. The mission was staffed by a missionary who preached to the Inuit each Sunday, and the church offered a warm place to rest, food, and other incentives to encourage attendance at services. This mission plays a significant role in Isuma's Nunavut series. In a key episode in the series, Isuma producer and cameraman Norman Cohn, the only non-Inuk among Isuma's leadership, plays the part of "Father Forehead," who tries to convert the Inuit to Christianity. The setting for the video is the actual mission, which still stands in Avaja and has become something of a tourist destination.

By the end of the 1930s, the Hudson's Bay Company had a permanent trading post in Igloolik. Ultimately, the stores operated by the HBC would become known as the "Northern" stores, and there is a Northern store in Igloolik to this day.

Inuit life has changed considerably since Atanarjuat's time; one significant factor in that shift involves the relocation of Inuit families and children. Starting in the 1930s, the Canadian government became increasingly interested in the Arctic. One impetus for this interest was territorial: other northern nations were beginning to send explorers, missionaries, and others into the upper reaches of North America, which raised concerns in Ottawa about the solidity of Canada's claim to the region. (As global warming heightens the possibility of shipping across the Northwest Passage, Canada is finding itself once again in the position of defending its governmental claim to the North American Arctic. The potential financial boon represented by an ice-free Northwest Passage is inspiring other nations to reassert their challenges to Canada's claim to the region.) To reinforce its sovereignty over the territory, Ottawa sent Royal Canadian Mounted Police patrols throughout the North. These officers were charged with enforcing Canadian laws, adjudicating disputes, and showing the Canadian flag to underscore Canada's claims to the area. Ottawa sought to construct other evidence of its authority as well. By the 1960s, Igloolik had an RCMP post, an elementary school, and a nursing station. All three are still functioning, and a high school has been added as well.

From the 1930s through the 1960s, Canadian officials also took steps to move the nomadic Inuit into more permanent settlements that were served by schools, clinics, and RCMP posts. This effort remains highly controversial. On the one hand, the steps were taken in response to legitimate concerns about starvation, disease, and other threats frequently faced by the Inuit. By moving these families into towns, the logic went, the Canadian government could more effectively serve and help them. On the other hand, the effort to relocate these families also stemmed from Ottawa's desire to assimilate Inuit into "mainstream" Canadian life. This desire grew partly from the sovereignty issue — it's hard to claim you have authority over a region if you do absolutely nothing for the people there — and partly from a belief that the Inuit way of life was somehow "backward," "dirty," and "heathen."

The relocation effort used several tools. One was the school system: Inuit children were forced to attend boarding schools sometimes hundreds of miles from home. At school the children were forbidden to speak Inuktitut, and they were often beaten or otherwise punished if they did so. (Kunuk attended one of these boarding schools, and to this day he bitterly resents the way he was treated there.) Another tool for relocation was government assistance. Families were told that if they allowed themselves to be moved to the settlements, they would receive food and other support from the government, but if they refused and remained on the land, they would be on their own. These pressures also came with promises of jobs, housing, and other benefits — which sometimes never materialized.

The relocation cost many Inuit their lives. Some found themselves in strange parts of the Arctic where they were unable to hunt successfully. Because hunting requires a deep knowledge of the land and the animals' migration patterns, moving a family to a new area often left them unable to find game. (There was some belief among the Canadian authorities that the Arctic is uniform from coast to coast, and so Inuit hunters would be successful anywhere.) Some Inuit died trying to walk hundreds of miles back to their homelands. Some died because the concentration of people in a settlement outstripped the land's ability to provide food for them; once the animals were overhunted, food quickly became scarce. Others caught diseases from living in close proximity with people from a wide range of locations.[2] The effects of the relocation and the agony it caused are still felt vividly today.

Igloolik Today

At the time of this writing, Igloolik has slightly more than 1,500 people. This represents a strong growth from the 1996 census, which recorded 1,174 people. Part of that growth is the result of the placement of several government offices in the community; those offices brought people and an influx of cash, and that boost to the economy attracted more people as well.

Physically, the town of Igloolik bears little resemblance to the site shown in *The Fast Runner*. Perhaps the most striking feature of the modern Igloolik skyline is the Igloolik Research Centre, which provides facilities for a wide range of scholars and other researchers doing fieldwork in the area. The building is a large disk mounted on a tall, narrow stalk, making it a distinctive feature on the generally flat Igloolik landscape; the design was intended to minimize heat transfer from the building to the ground below, to avoid melting the permafrost. Inside the stalk a curving staircase leads to the offices in the disk above, and windows all around the disk afford stunning views of Igloolik Island and the ocean. While the Research Centre represents a towering symbol of interest in Inuit culture, to some it also represents a continuation of Canadian — and American and European — domination over and manipulation of the Inuit for external and political gain. On several occasions Kunuk asked me why I was paying rent to the Canadian government for living and office space at the Research Centre when I could be staying with an Inuit family and paying my money to people in the community. In his usual enigmatic way, he once asked me how long I would be staying at the center. I said I was going to live in Igloolik for nine months, but then Norm Cohn intervened, explaining that Kunuk wasn't asking how long I would be in the Arctic. He was asking how long I planned to affiliate myself with the white, southern government of Canada. The question was not logistical but political. (For several reasons, I chose to stay at the center despite Kunuk's displeasure.)

Another eye-catching landmark is the town's airport. Situated on a slight ridge near the town, the airport building is painted bright blue and is easy to see from many angles. The major airline in the Nunavut region is First Air, which provides service to all the communities in the eastern Canadian Arctic. From cities throughout Canada, passengers can fly in comfortable jets to Iqaluit, the capital of Nunavut and the hub for the airline. Then small propeller planes seating several dozen people link to the outlying communities. These smaller planes carry an extensive amount of cargo as well as people; depending on the amount of cargo, seats can be removed and a divider can be placed anywhere on the plane. The cargo goes in the front section, with passengers occupying seats in the remaining space in back.

The original Catholic church in town is an impressive structure as well. Once it became clear that the town of Igloolik was going to become a population center, the Catholic Church abandoned its mission at Avaja and built a large stone church in Igloolik. The church is largely unused — a massive stone structure, it is very difficult to heat — but plans constantly swirl for one enterprise or another inside it. One idea would turn it into a pizza parlor; the pizza ovens would warm the place nicely.

Igloolik has three active churches: the St. Stephen Roman Catholic Church, the St. Matthias Anglican Church, and a small Pentecostal church. Services are performed in Inuktitut, although a more modern form of the language used in *The Fast Runner*. Hymns are sung in Inuktitut as well.

The characters in *The Fast Runner* had to live entirely off the land, but life in Igloolik has become much more comfortable — and safer — since then. Two stores in town, The Northern and the Co-op, provide a wide range of goods. Both sell an array of southern-style food, including TV dinners, canned soup and pasta dishes, and desserts, and both offer produce that is flown in with the regular plane service. The stores also sell clothing, rifles, games and toys, housewares, and almost anything else that Igloolik families might need. They even sell snowmobiles and ATVs.

The items for sale in the stores tend to be expensive by southern standards, because air shipping costs more than overland options would. (In the Arctic, there are no overland options.) But a cheaper approach is available. Once a year, a supply ship comes to the Nunavut region from southern Canada. It brings everything from bulk food items to cars and building supplies. Families in Igloolik calculate the quantities they need for the coming year of various staples — flour, baking soda, paper towels, tissues, batteries — and place an order well in advance. When the ship arrives, each family's bundle, loaded on a pallet and hauled by a forklift, is placed on the ground in front of the proper house. The family then rips open the plastic and hauls all the items inside, usually for storage in the suspended basement below their house.

In Atanarjuat's day, elders and shamans — and primarily women — dealt with all health issues, including diseases, injuries, and childbirth. In Igloolik today, health care is handled by a small clinic, which is staffed by a team of nurses. A doctor visits on a rotating schedule to take care of more serious needs and to conduct follow-up visits to monitor patients' conditions, and a dentist comes around from time to time to provide basic dental care. But any acute emergency care requires a Medivac trip in an air ambulance to Iqaluit or Montreal.

The camps that Atanarjuat and the others built are still in use in the Igloolik area, although the scene has changed somewhat. Instead of skin tents and igloos, families who are "out on the land" live in large canvas tents with wooden support poles. They use Coleman stoves for cooking and heating; these stoves are more efficient and easier to handle than the *qulliq* (the traditional half-moon-shaped stone lamp), although their use does represent a certain loss of charm. As in Atanarjuat's day, however, the families leave for their camps carrying very little food. They are confident in their knowledge of the land and the animals, and they know they will find food during their trip and around their camps. Most of the camps in the Igloolik region are in Iksivautaujaq, just beyond the point of land on the other side of Turton Bay from the town of Igloolik. Families travel to Iksivautaujaq by ATV in the summer and snowmobile in the winter.

During the four thousand years that people have been living in the Igloolik area, families have always camped year-round at Iksivautaujaq. Archaeological teams have found foundations for ancient sod houses and other evidence showing occupation dating back millennia. The winter of 1998–1999, however, marked the first known time in which no people camped at Iksivautaujaq. The last of the families had come to town to enroll their children in the school and to take advantage of other services the town could offer. It seems that a four thousand–year history of continuous occupation was broken during the darkness of that winter.

Today, families set up their canvas tents and leave them in place, marking their favorite camping spots. Most are at Iksivautaujaq, but others are near the town, at a place called Ham Bay. (Kunuk has a campsite there.) Ham Bay is an excellent fishing spot in the summer, and campers use nets to catch good numbers of tasty Arctic char. The fish are gutted on the beach and hung on racks to dry in the sun.

One of the main reasons families continue to camp in the areas outside of town is that life takes on a different pace there. In town, life is governed by the clock. School starts at a certain time, stores open and close on a prescribed schedule, television programs begin on the half-hour, and so on. When you are "out on the land," however, you live more as Atanarjuat and his companions did — you follow your own internal clock. You eat when you're hungry and sleep when you're tired; there are no predetermined mealtimes or bedtimes. Because the sun stays in the sky twenty-four hours a day in the summer — and never rises at all for seven weeks in the winter — you are free to listen to your own rhythms. Many of the people around Igloolik deeply appreciate the chance to relax and liberate themselves from the rigid routines of town life.

In *The Fast Runner*, hunters and families traveled by dogsled often, but today, few people use dog teams. In general, dog teams are so impractical compared to snowmobiles that people have abandoned them. According to Canadian law, however, all polar bear hunting must be done by dogsled; the intent of the law was to maintain a level of knowledge about how to raise dogs for pulling and how to operate a dogsled successfully. The law seems to have been effective. Around Igloolik, a small number of families raise dogs for pulling and keep a sled or two on hand. When hunters from the South make arrangements to hunt for polar bears, these dog-team owners break out their gear and take the hunters out on the land. If it weren't for that thin connection to this ancient tradition, the knowledge of dog-team driving might well be lost for good.

Video in Igloolik

Today, the community of Igloolik is unique in many ways. It is generally considered the most traditional of the Nunavut communities, meaning that it retains more of the old ways of life — igloo building, dog-team handling, and so forth — than do the other communities.

It also is the home to three video organizations, all of which create videos and programs that express Inuit culture in various ways. Thanks to *The Fast Runner* and their other works, Igloolik Isuma Productions is the best known of the three. But while the other two approach video work from very different perspectives, they are nevertheless active and successful themselves.

The Inuit Broadcasting Corporation was founded in 1981 as a direct response to an organized Inuit movement against television in the North. Because of the vast distances involved, television comes to Arctic communities by satellite. Communities that choose to accept television install large satellite dishes that receive the signals and send them by cable to the homes in town. This system allows each community to decide whether to accept television or not.

Igloolik was the last community in the Arctic to accept television. It rejected the offer twice previously, both times on the grounds that television would erode Inuit languages and traditions. *Iglulingmiut* (people in Igloolik) were concerned that if children watched a lot of programming from southern Canada, the United States, and Europe, they would come to consider southern values and languages superior to their own.

In an effort to link the North with southern Canada more closely, using new broadcast technologies, the Canadian government launched an experiment to see whether satellite programming would work in the Arctic. Called the Anik project, the experiment found that satellite broadcasting could be worthwhile and cost-effective in the North. After some initial adjustments in approach, a system was approved that would use satellites to bring television and radio to communities that voted to receive them. In addition, in response to concerns about cultural erosion and imperialism, the Canadian government created the IBC to create and distribute television programming in the Inuktitut language and with a focus on northern issues. With the creation of the IBC and assurances that it would create and carry programming in Inuktitut, Igloolik consented to receive television in 1981.[3]

The IBC is headquartered in Ottawa, near the governmental funding sources that finance it. The main production office, however, is located in Iqaluit, the capital of Nunavut and the territory's largest city. Several communities have IBC production offices: Baker Lake, Igloolik, Iqaluit, Rankin Inlet, and Taloyoak. Each center creates programming that it feeds to the main hub in Iqaluit; the material is then packaged for the various programs that the IBC broadcasts.

Igloolik is responsible for much of the IBC's cultural programming. The producers in the Igloolik office create videos for several of the IBC's shows, but these videos tend not to focus on cultural re-creations, as Isuma's products often do. Instead, they offer insights and information about the cultural activities going on today: drum dancing, ceremonies, caribou hunting, and the like.

The IBC broadcasts several popular shows. *Kippingujautiit* (Things to Pass Time By) is a half-hour show for adults that entertains with funny stories, musical performances, coverage of games and events, and information about Inuit cultural practices past and present. (The Igloolik center provides much of this programming.) *Qaggik* (Drum Dance in an Igloo) is a half-hour program that focuses on news and current events. *Qanuq Isumavit?* (What Do You Think?) is a live call-in program that focuses on current events. Inuktitut is used throughout the show. *Qaujisaut* (To See, To Find Out) offers entertaining material designed to help young Inuit who feel caught between two cultures. *Takuginai* (Look Here) is a children's show that features Johnny the Lemming and other puppets. The focus of the program is Inuit cultural values, including respect for elders and patience. The program also teaches basic Inuktitut, much as *Sesame Street* teaches basic English.

The IBC has played a significant role in the advancement of Native media in Canada. In addition to its own efforts to produce programming in Inuktitut from an Inuit perspective, the IBC is a founding member of Television Northern Canada (TVNC). TVNC was launched in 1992 to provide a dedicated satellite channel on which Native programming could be shown. The channel was offered as an optional service on cable television carriers, and because the signal was not scrambled, it also made Native programming available throughout Canada for viewers who had satellite receivers. TVNC was considered the primary distributor of Native programming to northern Canada.

The IBC also is a founding member of APTN, the Aboriginal Peoples Television Network. APTN stemmed from a desire to broadcast Native material throughout Canada, giving people in the southern cities an opportunity to learn about their country's more northern peoples. In 1999, TVNC was expanded to include national distribution, including mandatory inclusion in the basic package offered by all cable carriers, and it was renamed APTN.

APTN primarily broadcasts material from Canada's Native groups, but it also includes Native material from around the world.

Tariagsuk Video Centre

The other video organization in Igloolik is the Tariagsuk Video Centre, a community-oriented, walk-in video center that offers training and equipment to anyone in Igloolik who would like to produce videos.

The center was founded by Marie-Hélène Cousineau; she is Norman Cohn's partner, and she lives in Montreal and Igloolik. She started the center to give people in the community a chance to make videos about topics that were important to them.

With the help of Igloolik Isuma and some government grants, the center opened in 1991. Shortly after that debut, several women got together with Cousineau to form Arnait Ikajurtigiit, a women's video group. The group, now called Arnait Productions, gives its members the chance to make videos that share their particular point of view. At first the group met at various members' houses and taped each other preparing food, sewing, or taking part in other household activities. This effort allowed the group to gain expertise with the camera and editing equipment, and it also brought the women together to discuss the kind of major projects they wanted to tackle.

One of Arnait's first projects was a video series about childbirth and health issues for women. The series consists of women interviewing female elders about how they handled childbirth and other issues out on the land.

One of the most prominent projects undertaken by Arnait was a video titled *Ataguttaaluk*. Ataguttaaluk was a leader in the Igloolik area in the early twentieth century. She went off with her husband, her children, and some friends on a hunting trip one summer, but game was scarce. As they continued to look for food, the members of the party grew weaker, and some died. As winter made their situation bleak, some of the dying members of the group, including Ataguttaaluk's husband, invited the others to eat their bodies after they had passed away. In traditional Inuit culture, it is important that at least one person survive any ordeal so that he or she can tell others what had happened.

Cannibalism is a serious taboo in Inuit culture, as it is in many other parts of the world. But when circumstances are dire, people sometimes resort to eating human flesh in an effort to survive. Ataguttaaluk and the other remaining members of the group ate the flesh of their friends and relatives in a desperate attempt to hold on until spring.

In the end, Ataguttaaluk was the only survivor. She was discovered by a passing hunting party in the spring, and she was nursed back to health. She honored the list of taboos that accompany the eating of the dead — she remained in her tent most of the time, severely limiting her contact with others for an entire year. Eventually, she was welcomed back into Igloolik society, and she went on to become a prominent leader of the community. Today, both the elementary school and the high school are named for her.

To make the video, the women of Arnait asked the oldest elder in town, Rosie Ukkumaluk, to tell Ataguttaaluk's story. They set up the video camera in Ukkumaluk's living room and filmed the entire twenty-three-minute telling of the tale. The intent was to provide multiple layers of meaning: the importance of survival, the inspiration of Ataguttaaluk's story, and the value of elders and the wisdom they possess. By showing Ukkumaluk telling the Ataguttaaluk legend, the Arnait producers were able to convey more than just the starvation story line.

Another important Arnait video is *Itivimiut*, meaning "People of the Other Side." Igloolik and Pond Inlet have long had a close relationship, and travelers from one community would often make the trek overland, a trip of several days by snowmobile and much longer by dogsled, to visit the people "on the other side." Typically, however, it was either men or families that made the voyage, with the men taking responsibility for all the necessary hunting. The women of Arnait wanted to show that women were perfectly capable of living off the land, so they decided to make the journey themselves — without men. They took along their video gear to document the trip, and arrived in Pond Inlet without difficulty. The video shows the resourcefulness and the camaraderie of the women as they cross the long stretch between communities together.

The Tariagsuk Video Centre broadcasts a call-in program devoted to news and current affairs that brings the people of Igloolik together into discussions about important events in the region. But Arnait Productions remains the most productive facet of the Tariagsuk Video Center. *Before Tomorrow*, the group's first major film, was released early in 2008. Based on the novel *For Morgendagen*, by Danish writer Jørn Riel, the film tells the story of a grandmother and grandson struggling to survive together in the North.

Two Worlds

Many Inuit today talk about the need they feel to negotiate two distinct worlds. They live in frame houses and watch television, but they also hunt on the land and eat the foods their ancestors ate. They drive ATVs and snowmobiles, but they also spend time in outpost camps that have been occupied for centuries. They enjoy the conveniences of washing machines, refrigerators, and stoves, but they also place seals on the floor for people to eat from when they're hungry.

Isuma functions in both worlds as well. The Isuma producers create videos that bring cutting-edge technology to bear on the ancient art of Inuit storytelling. They depict people from Atanarjuat's time — five hundred years ago — and they show the new generation of Inuit leaders who are reshaping, for better or worse, the nature of Inuit life. And they pursue their work in a modern studio but with an appreciation of long-standing Inuit rhythms of living and interacting.

Isuma embraces Inuit values as they existed in the past and as they exist in the present. Video gives the producers a means by which they can honor the wisdom and ethos of their elders while at the same time making a statement about the relevance and worth of Inuit today. Through the retelling, in video form, of ancient Inuit legends — and through demonstrating time-honed approaches to everyday life in the Arctic, as they do in many of their other videos — the Isuma producers are able to combine multiple contexts into a coherent and important set of messages.

Modern contexts allow Isuma to create videos and share them with the world. Ancient Inuit traditions and culture give Isuma rich messages and compelling content. Between them — and to an extent because of them — *The Fast Runner* and other Isuma videos offer perspectives on Inuit life that inform and inspire viewers beyond the beaches of Igloolik.

CHAPTER TWO

Seeing the Unseen

Zacharias Kunuk and the other Isuma producers went to great lengths to make *The Fast Runner* ethnographically true. They consulted elders about language, relationships, clothing, implements, and other facets of Inuit life represented in the film. They considered multiple versions of the oral legend circulating in the North. And they wrote the screenplay with attention to detail and authenticity to the best of their ability.

In addition to physical and social authenticity, the Isuma producers also sought spiritual authenticity. Kunuk takes spiritual powers quite seriously, and many of his works offer glimpses into the unseen realm. For example, in *Saputi*, a video about building a weir to catch fish in a river, Kunuk allows the story line to drift away from fishing and into the spirit world, which becomes close and powerful during times of physical inactivity.

Much of the conflict in *The Fast Runner* is carried out either on the spiritual plane or with the intervention of spiritual powers. An understanding of the spiritual context within which the film was made is essential for a full grasp of the film's significance. Just as Greek myths depict people as the puppets — and, at times, the beneficiaries, tools, and victims — of the gods and their Olympian struggles, *The Fast Runner* pursues its story arc in both the human and the spiritual spheres.

The first intervention of the spirit world in the movie occurs in the opening scene, when Sauri, coveting his father's role as camp leader, invites the evil shaman Tuurngarjuaq into the generally peaceful and prosperous camp. (For a brief rundown of the overall plot, see chapter five.) The audience isn't shown how Sauri contacted Tuurngarjuaq and enticed him to play a destructive role in the camp's social structure, but the disturbing shaman arrives at the igloo where most of the families are visiting with each other. Before long, a contest is arranged between Tuurngarjuaq and the successful and popular camp leader Kumaglak.

Both men are shamans, meaning they have developed special powers involving the spirit world. In preparation for the contest, each shaman is bound tightly in ropes, which limits his ability to compete on the human plane and forces the competition into the spirit realm. Both men draw heavily on their spiritual resources; their grunting and contorted expressions, reflecting walrus and polar bear spirit helpers, indicate that the battle is fierce, and largely removed from ordinary human perception. Ultimately, Tuurngarjuaq prevails — and Kumaglak loses his life in the struggle.

For a long time after that clash, in which Tuurngarjuaq declared that Sauri would be the new head of the camp, the Igloolik families go about their business with little conspicuous involvement with the spirit world. Qulitalik and his wife leave Igloolik, aware that Tuurngarjuaq's powers are formidable. Panikpak, another shaman, remains behind; she is Qulitalik's sister, and she promises to contact him "in her heart" when the time is right for his return.

The camp after the battle is run through politics and force, rather than through harmonious relations with the spirit world. Sauri had arranged the murder of his father by bringing in a powerful shaman, but his own son, Uqi, murders Sauri by stabbing him with a knife. Atanarjuat's family suffers throughout this time, marginalized first by Sauri and then by Uqi, but they respond by working hard and trying to live cheerfully.

It is the murderous assault on Atanarjuat and his brother that begins to reintroduce shamanistic powers and spiritual connections into the camp. Uqi and his gang attack Atanarjuat and his brother, Aamarjuaq, but just as Uqi is about to stab through the tent wall to kill Atanarjuat a voice distracts the killers. The script describes the scene:

Bloodthirsty and desperate, the attackers stab frantically at any shape. Uqi sights Atanarjuat and moves in slowly for the kill. A ghostly VOICE *calls out an urgent warning...*

VOICE (OS) Atanarjuat angajuata aqpakpasii! Atanarjuat's
brother is running after you!
*The attackers freeze. Uqi whirls around behind him. His murder-
ing face is bestial, feral, his eyes a bloody red. Uqi's POV: he finds
himself face to face with his long-dead grandfather, the murdered
Kumaglak. Totally real. The ghost points its finger.*
KUMAGLAK'S GHOST: Uqi!
*Uqi throws his spear through the figure, which then disappears.
He stares dumbfounded. Behind him, from under the far corner of
the collapsed tent, Atanarjuat scrambles out. Completely naked,
he jumps to his feet and takes off running as fast as he can without
looking back. Uqi whips his head back around to see Atanarjuat
escaping.*
PAKAK: There he goes!
Uqi grabs Pakak's spear and takes off after Atanarjuat. (Igloolik
Isuma Productions 2002, 103–4)

In this moment of extreme danger — not only for Atanarjuat, but
also for the health and safety of the entire community — Kumaglak
reappears to change the course of events. His shamanistic powers
were not enough to protect him from Tuurngarjuaq, but he is able
to return to the earthly realm long enough to thwart Uqi's plan to
kill Atanarjuat. The distraction he introduces allows Atanarjuat to
escape and begin his torturous dash across the ice.

The original shamanistic battle, between Kumaglak and Tuurngarjuaq, has now been taken up again. Tuurngarjuaq is still around —
the camp has been peaceful largely because no one has been able
to challenge his spiritual power — but new heroes are needed to
replace the fallen Kumaglak. Kumaglak's return to save Atanarjuat's
life triggers a series of events that culminate in just such a realign-
ment of forces.

We see the intervention of spiritual powers later during Atanarjuat's run across the ice. Such a desperate move — running naked
and barefoot across the ice toward the tiny island of Sioraq — would
have been fatal for most people. But Atanarjuat is extraordinarily fast
on his feet, which allows him to widen the gap between himself and

the pursuing killers. He would have been doomed, however, were it not for a wide crack in the ice, called a lead — one of many that interrupt the ice between Igloolik and Sioraq. As Atanarjuat sprints toward the lead, he judges it too far for a man to jump across. But as he approaches, he sees a person on the other side, waving him on: "Jump! Jump!" With this encouragement, and with no other way to escape his pursuers, Atanarjuat dashes toward the lead and hurls himself into the air. He lands on the other side — "miraculously," says the script — but the figure who urged him to jump has disappeared. He was another materialization of the spirit world, helping Atanarjuat stay alive. The appearance of this figure and Atanarjuat's successful jump across the lead reinforce the idea that spiritual forces representing the side of good are working to help Atanarjuat restore balance to the community.

The interventions of the spirit world in the realm of human affairs continue. Qulitalik, the shaman who left Igloolik with his wife and adopted daughter when Sauri took over the camp, is especially attuned to the signs and meanings of the spirit world. He senses Atanarjuat's arrival in a vague but tangible way, and he asks his daughter to cook extra food, "so no one will be hungry." When she teases him about expecting guests on isolated Sioraq, he "smiles and shakes his head, as if to say 'you never know.'" He has already felt the fleeting indicators of something momentous coming, and he scans the distant ice often. It is that premonition that allows him to spot Atanarjuat on the ice and get him to the safety of the camp at Sioraq.

That safety exists only on the human plane, however. Even after Uqi and his sidekicks poke around camp and then leave, frustrated in their search for Atanarjuat's body, Qulitalik can tell that the larger struggle is only just beginning. "It's worse than you think," he says to Atanarjuat, without explanation.

Qulitalik's intimacy with the spirit world allows him to grasp that Atanarjuat's appearance represents the first step toward the restoration of harmony in Igloolik — the driving out of the evil shaman and his disruptive forces. Qulitalik knows the challenges that such an endeavor holds, and he is not certain of the outcome. He is concerned that Atanarjuat fails to understand the situation. Atanarjuat seems to think he should rest, regain his strength, and confront Uqi. But Qulitalik knows that the real test lies in defeating not Uqi but Tuurngarjuaq, and he knows that Atanarjuat must be prepared for that battle as well.

> QULITALIK You don't even notice something is still after you.
> ATANARJUAT (*alarmed*) What do you mean? Is someone coming?
> QULITALIK It's already here.
> ATANARJUAT I thought I saw something out there today . . . Is there a bear around?
> QULITALIK (*exasperated*) You have a lot more to worry about than bears! (Igloolik Isuma Productions 2002, 133)

Throughout the rest of the time on Sioraq, Qulitalik reads signs and interprets events in an effort to discern what to do and how to ensure success.

When the showdown between Atanarjuat and Tuurngarjuaq looms, Qulitalik tries to prepare Atanarjuat as much as possible. He repeatedly tells him to be ready for battle on more than one level: "You'll need more than strong feet when the spirits start whispering in your ears." At last, Qulitalik makes it plain: "You know what's out there when you're all alone. Are you ready to face that?"

Atanarjuat finally realizes that he must confront not just Uqi but Tuurngarjuaq as well, and that negating Tuurngarjuaq's power will be essential if he is to defeat Uqi. He decides to go out on the land by himself to face Tuurngarjuaq, and Qulitalik gives him some tools imbued with special powers: a walrus-skin pouch, in which he must place the droppings of every animal he sees; a rock, which he must carry in his left hand until he knows what to do with it; a rabbit's foot. He tells Atanarjuat to bring the pouch and the rabbit's foot back to him after his upcoming trials add to their power. As explained in the published screenplay, "In Inuit culture, excrement (anaq) is much more than body waste. It is a dynamic link in the chain of life from the animal world, through the human body, and back to the environment. It has a strong symbolic value. . . . It should therefore be no surprise that animal excrement, beginning with dog dung, was used in shamanism" (Igloolik Isuma Productions 2002, 145).

The three-way clash among good spirits, evil spirits, and humans comes to a boil as Atanarjuat departs. He comes upon a dead bear, which turns out to be Tuurngarjuaq in creatural form. The beast knocks Atanarjuat down and nearly kills him, but the rock that Qulitalik gave him holds powerful shamanistic potency. Atanarjuat is able to use the rock to free himself from the hideous monster.

At night, Atanarjuat is beset by nightmares, flashes of images containing the power of physical contests, passionate lovemaking, and familial bonds. He is haunted by images of people alive and dead: his wife Atuat, who accuses him of abandoning her; Kumaglak, their son, who cries for his father; and Aamarjuaq, his murdered brother, who blames Atanarjuat for his death. Tuurngarjuaq, unsuccessful at beating Atanarjuat in a physical clash, is resorting to mental and emotional torture to wear his opponent down.

The ultimate test, however, comes when Tuurngarjuaq disguises himself as Qulitalik and chats with Atanarjuat out on the ice, strangely far from Sioraq. As Qulitalik, he appears calm and benevolent. He offers reassuring congratulations to Atanarjuat, then asks for his pouch and rabbit's foot. But he tries to grab them just a little too quickly, and Atanarjuat becomes suspicious and pulls them back. Tuurngarjuaq screams in rage and reverts to his man-beast form. He rams his harpoon into Atanarjuat's chest. Atanarjuat falls to the ground, but he still holds the amulets. By clinging to the powers of good, Atanarjuat is able to prevail against Tuurngarjuaq's plots.

The final great intervention of the spirit world in the realm of human affairs comes at the end of the film. Atanarjuat has made his human plans — hunting extra meat, fashioning crampons and a club out of caribou antlers to give him the advantage in the final show-down with Uqi and his men — but he has also reached a spiritual understanding. Through the patient teachings of Qulitalik and the confrontation with Tuurngarjuaq on the ice, Atanarjuat has moved from a strictly human perspective to a view that encompasses the spiritual plane as well. He understands that his struggle is not only against Uqi and not only against Tuurngarjuaq; he must also find a way to end the cycle of evil.

When Atanarjuat returns to Igloolik with Qulitalik and his family, he functions primarily on the human plane. He greets his family, exacts a bit of personal revenge against his evil wife, Puja, and pretends to be gracious to his former attackers. But shamanistic powers are still at work. Qulitalik had sent a spirit rabbit to Igloolik in advance of their arrival, and Uqi caught it and ate it all himself. Now Uqi is acting strangely. When Atanarjuat confronts him in an ice-slicked igloo, Uqi puts up a strong fight, but without the direct participation of Tuurngarjuaq and his evil force, Uqi ultimately is defeated. Atanarjuat, however, despite having the clear advantage in the fight, declines to kill Uqi. After demonstrating his superiority as a fighter, Atanarjuat ends the feud by refusing to kill his rival.

Tuurngarjuaq must now be driven from Igloolik for good. He is powerful; he was able to kill Kumaglak in the opening shamanistic contest. But Qulitalik has been preparing for this moment for some time. Qulitalik positions himself in the igloo, sends all the children away, and then grunts out a challenge like a bull walrus.

The challenge is audible beyond the human sphere, and before long Tuurngarjuaq arrives, ready for battle. But circumstances are different now; this is not the same camp that he poisoned with his evil thirty years previously. Opposite him is Qulitalik, not Kumaglak — and Qulitalik knows what he is up against. Kumaglak was caught off guard, but Qulitalik is prepared for the evil shaman's power. Atanarjuat's family and friends are prepared as well; they are ready to drive this monster out for good.

When Tuurngarjuaq arrives, Qulitalik holds up the walrus-skin pouch in which Atanarjuat gathered the droppings of many animals. This is not a lone walrus spirit fighting Tuurngarjuaq. Spirit helpers in many forms are joined in the battle. Human helpers are willing to fight as well, and they join Qulitalik in his grunting like "a herd of threatening animals."

And Qulitalik is not the only powerful shaman on the side of good. Panikpak, Qulitalik's sister and the widow of the murdered Kumaglak, has powers of her own, and she rises to join her brother in this confrontation. When the tensions reach their climax, Qulitalik showers Tuurngarjuaq with dust from the pouch; multiple spirit powers invade his body at once. He begins to bleed and fall apart, and then a blast of wind knocks him out of the human world forever.

With the evil eliminated and the authority of the proper elders now returned, Qulitalik and Panikpak take their rightful place as the leaders of the camp. They turn their attention back to the human plane as Panikpak announces the banishment of Uqi, Puja, and their helpers.

Shamans, Amulets, and Talismans

The actions of the shamans and their spirit helpers represent an important facet of the supernatural forces at work in the legend and in the movie. As explained in a sidebar in the published version of the *Fast Runner* screenplay,

> A shaman is a mediator between the human world and the spirit world, between the living and the dead, and between animals and human society. A future shaman must be chosen by a spirit — maybe one of his deceased parents, maybe his namesake, maybe an animal whose skin was used to wipe his newborn body, or maybe any spirit that has appeared to him. . . . The spirits of the polar bear and the walrus were especially sought after. Their size and their ability to move in water and on land made them powerful mediators. (Igloolik Isuma Productions 2002, 39)

Spiritual powers are also manifest in the attributes of the main characters. Atanarjuat is able to escape his pursuers because he is a fast runner. His brother, Aamarjuaq, has great strength. But these brothers did not come by their skills through luck. They possess these traits because their mother had the foresight to take the necessary steps to endow her sons with their skills.

In traditional Inuit belief systems, powers come from the spirit world but are represented on the earthly plane by animals. A mother who wanted her son to be strong, for example, might wear an amulet made of muscle or the bone of a strong animal, such as a walrus or a bear. While pregnant, she might also eat the meat of strong animals in preference to weaker ones, choosing bear or walrus over caribou or birds. Similarly, she might eat caribou if she wanted her son to be a fast runner, and she might wear an amulet made of caribou tendon to bring fleetness to her child. For several weeks after birth, the infant might be adorned with an amulet representing the desired traits.

The mother of Atanarjuat and Aamarjuaq took specific steps necessary to give her sons certain advantages. As part of the oral history project for elders being conducted in Igloolik, Zachariasie Panippakuttuk described how the brothers got their strength and speed:

I have heard a legend about Aamajjuaq and Atanaarjuat who were the two brothers. It is said that both had different *pigusiq* [amulet]. The older brother Aamarjuaq was said to have a *pigusiq* of a walrus fore limb so that he will be strong, as for the younger brother Atanaarjuat he had pigusiq of caribou muscles so that he can be a fast runner. But I know for certain that these held truth as it is said that Aamarjuaq was a strong person while Atanaarjuat was a fast runner. The legend itself has a lot of truth in it. (Panippakuttuk 1991)

These approaches embrace the idea of contagious magic, which involves the transmission of powers through physical contact. By touching walrus muscle or eating walrus meat, the power of strength that the walrus possesses is transferred to the recipient. Similarly, contact with caribou meat or sinew will make a person run swiftly.

Another conspicuous element of spiritual power in the film

involves connections with spirit helpers who take on animal forms. In traditional Inuit culture, many people developed relationships with spirit helpers that would assist them both in the spirit realm and on Earth. Typically, these relationships would come about not by the person seeking a particular spirit helper but rather through the initiated action of the helper. The helper spirit presents itself in a conspicuous way to the person, who then understands that the relationship has begun. A spirit helper finds you, not the other way around.

The primary way that a spirit helper can assist a person is through the granting of certain abilities associated with that animal. A caribou spirit helper might help a person run quickly or sense danger from afar. A snowy owl might help someone see great distances. The animals fall into a loose hierarchy, with the walrus and the polar bear, the two strongest and most formidable animals, at the top. On the material plane, these two animals have no natural predators (other than humans). In fact, a fight between a polar bear and a walrus is generally considered an equal match. In *The Fast Runner*, Tuurngarjuaq relies on his polar bear spirit helper, but he is countered in both the beginning, with Kumaglak, and the ending, with Qulitalik and Panikpak, by walrus spirit helpers. Those choices are not accidental. If a shaman with a weaker spirit helper battled another shaman with a polar bear, the former would most likely lose.

Shamanism and the animistic belief system associated with it have largely vanished from Inuit life, at least on the surface. The evangelical work of Jesuit, Anglican, and other religious missionaries has brought about a strong Christian faith in the Arctic, and with that shift came a marked dwindling of shamanism. Igloolik has a Catholic church, an Anglican church, and a Pentecostal church, and most of the people in town identify with one of these faiths.

But shamanism is not entirely dead. When I first inquired about shamanism in Igloolik, I was told that it is long gone, relegated to the make-believe world of superstition and magic. The story of its demise is fairly uniform. When the missionaries came to the Arctic, the story goes, the existing animistic belief system had many deities. Sedna, for example (also known as Arnakuagsak, Arnarquagssaq, Nerrivik, Nuliajuk, and Arnapkapfaaluk, and by other names), is a woman who lives at the bottom of the sea and controls the movements of all sea mammals; by bringing the seals, whales, walruses, and polar bears close to her, she can bring about starvation for the Inuit who rely on those animals for food.[1] Silap Inua (or Silla), the god of the moon, controls the weather and other powerful forces. Other major deities influenced Inuit life in many ways, which often entailed the observance of a complex and strict system of taboos.

In addition to the major deities, all living things were believed to be possessed by a soul and hence worthy of spiritual respect. And for some Inuit, even inanimate objects — rocks, the sea, and so forth — were sentient and soulful as well.

When the missionaries arrived, the Inuit listened to them talk about Jesus and the promise of a glorious afterlife.[2] Those who liked what they heard, and those who liked the material opportunities the missionaries provided, including rifles, food, and a warm place to spend Sunday morning, simply added Jesus to the panoply of deities already in place. Eventually, through attendance at church, the translation of the Bible into the Inuktitut syllabary, and other efforts, the shamanistic animism was left behind.

Despite that narrative, however, and despite the frequent declaration that all Inuit have abandoned traditional spiritualism in favor of Christianity, there are still people in the Arctic who claim shamanistic powers. The days of people holding the profession of shaman are essentially gone, but when good and trusting relationships are formed, a fair number of Inuit will maintain that they possess some kind of shamanistic power.

After I had lived in Igloolik for some time, one person told me about a shamanistic ritual by which questions could be answered. The example he gave: "In which direction should we travel to find walrus to hunt?" He would lie on the floor or a bed and place a towel or other piece of fabric beneath his head. The question would be asked with a specific potential answer: "Should we travel in this direction to find walrus?" Then the spectators would lift the towel. If his head rose easily, bending at the neck, then the answer was no. A new direction would be indicated and the question asked again. This would continue until the shaman's body stayed rigid when the towel was lifted. His chin did not tilt toward his chest; rather, his neck was stiff and solid. That was a "yes" answer.

According to the person who described this procedure, the shaman lying down does not have to know the answer in advance. (If he did, there would be little point to the ritual; someone would just ask him the question and receive an honest reply.) Many people have shamanistic powers at this level, he said. It works with a lot of people.

Another informant deflected my questions about shamanism until later in my relationship with him. Then he told me about Inuktitut words and how they possess powers if given to you by a shaman who "owns" them. He then gave me a word and explained that it would have power for me whenever I chose to use it.

Shamanism, then, is not altogether gone from the Arctic. It is not considered appropriate in the modern age to admit that you are a shaman, but some people will do so if they trust the people around them. Interestingly, it has never been considered desirable to be a shaman. Most people who discovered they had shamanistic abilities were ashamed to tell their families. In general, it meant you were doomed to live off the gifts of others, because instead of hunting or taking care of your family, you were destined to perform shamanistic acts in exchange for food or other donations. That reluctance persists today, in stronger fashion, now that Christianity has become the dominant religion in the North.

This understanding of shamanism adds an interesting note to the characters in the movie. Typically, shamanistic powers were considered neutral; they were not good or evil in themselves but could be used for good or evil purposes. Like much of science, the raw knowledge carried no value judgments with it, but the abilities it embraced could be used in a variety of ways for a wide range of purposes.

In *The Fast Runner*, Tuurngarjuaq is an embodiment of pure evil. No ambiguity resides in him. He represents ill intent, disruption, the violation of taboos. In the final major scene in the film, the screenplay describes the yelping of Tuurngarjuaq's dogs and declares: "The Devil's dogteam stops outside the door." Tuurngarjuaq is a kind of Satan, a purely malevolent force that brings temporary benefits only to those who succumb to its lures.

That portrayal moves the film further into the potent and intriguing world of myth. Whereas in real life, a shaman might be a good person or an obnoxious one, each encompassing the full gray scale of human absurdities, in the mythical realm power can be drawn from simplicity. In a titanic clash between Good and Evil, the protagonist must be fully heroic and the antagonist must be fully villainous. By representing Tuurngarjuaq as pure evil — and Atanarjuat, Qulitalik, and others as full members of the good side — the film moves away from the human realm shown by the interactions of camp life and closer to the kind of Olympian struggles seen in many Greek tragedies.

CHAPTER THREE

The People and the Path of Isuma

Igloolik Isuma Productions is a loose collection of people. It expands when funding comes in and a project is under way, then contracts again when projects end and the group applies for the next production grant. In its largest formation — for example, during work on *The Fast Runner* and *Rasmussen* — it employs dozens of people: actors, costumers, makeup artists, set and prop builders, dog-team wranglers, and so on. When those projects ended, most of the people involved in production went back to their regular lives in Igloolik. The magic of Isuma is that it grows directly out of the community when it expands: all the people are ordinary citizens of the town who pitch in when a large project comes along.

At its inception, the core of Isuma consisted of four people: Zacharias Kunuk, Norman Cohn, Pauloosie Qulitalik, and Paul Apak. When Apak passed away in 1998, the group shrank to three, with additional writers, assistants, and others brought in as needed.

Zacharias Kunuk

At the heart of the Isuma enterprise is Zacharias Kunuk, one of the founders of Isuma and the primary producer. Kunuk was born in an outpost camp in 1957 and grew up in the Igloolik area. When he was in town, he enjoyed watching movies that were shown in the school's gym; for a quarter, he could watch John Wayne westerns and other classic films.

Like many Inuit children of his generation, he was taken away to boarding school to learn English and become more like "mainstream" Canadians. He remembers that period in his life bitterly. Nuns would beat him when he spoke Inuktitut, but he arrived knowing no English at all. As a result, for most of his time at the boarding school, he spoke very little.

When he returned to Igloolik, he spent his time hunting and carving sculptures. He became a skilled artist, and his carvings commanded considerable sums on the art market. But he still enjoyed movies greatly, and he was delighted when he heard that video gear had become small enough and cheap enough for ordinary people to own and use.

When he told me the story of how he got started in videography, his voice carried the tone of experience; he has told this story many times before. In 1981, before anyone in Igloolik had a television, Kunuk made some carvings and took them to Montreal. He could already see that videography — moviemaking — was a new art form that inexpensive video equipment made accessible, and he was interested in using his success as a carver to launch an exploration into this new medium. He sold his carvings in the city and found a store that carried video equipment. He bought a complete set: camera, VCR, and television. The store clerk showed him how to turn everything on and which button to push to record. Then Kunuk flew back to Igloolik to try out his newfound art.

At first, he shot footage of his son crawling on the floor and playing with his toys. When he played the images back on his TV, he said, he heard some noises behind him. He turned around to discover a large knot of children pressed up against his windows, fascinated by the flickering images they saw on the screen.

When the Inuit Broadcasting Corporation opened a production center in Igloolik, Kunuk joined them as a videographer and producer. The IBC brought in some videographers from the South to train the new producers. Among them was the experimental videographer Norman Cohn. Cohn was flown to Iqaluit for a workshop, and Kunuk signed up to take it.

The two hit it off from the start. While the workshop was winding down, Cohn and Kunuk wandered around Iqaluit shooting footage for a video they called *Two Strangers in Frobisher Bay*.[1] Cohn taught Kunuk about camera angles, video grammar, and the importance of immersing yourself in the scene, even if it feels uncomfortable to walk up and stick a camera in someone's face.

Kunuk's second independent video was called *From Inuk Point of View*. It shows his family, various activities around Igloolik, and other scenes, all with a voice-over in Inuktitut. Kunuk began to think seriously about a long-term career in videography. He worked with the IBC for nine years, ultimately becoming the chief producer.

Norman Cohn

Norman Cohn is the only non-Inuk principal of Isuma, a situation that raises eyebrows in some circles. Some people wonder how Isuma can call itself an Inuit video outfit when one of the two primary producers is a Caucasian from Montreal.

When I asked him that question, Cohn was prepared with an answer. Sitting in the kitchen of his small house in Igloolik, drinking coffee during a torrential rainstorm in the brief darkness of the September Arctic night, Cohn told me that being Inuit is not a matter of blood quantum. It is not about who your grandparents were or what your skin looks like. It is about how fully you embrace Inuit culture and adopt Inuit perspectives. When Cohn came to the Arctic and met Kunuk, he felt a strong connection with the rhythms and approaches of Inuit life. He listened and learned about Inuit views, Inuit attitudes, and Inuit values. And he devoted his videographic talents to the sharing of Inuit stories and activities.

Authenticity comes in two kinds, external and internal. External authenticity deals with surface appearances: does that "Navajo" bracelet fit in with the Navajo bracelets that came before it? Is it made of materials that are often used in Navajo jewelry? Does it have a similar look, an aesthetic that resonates with the existing body of Navajo art?

Internal authenticity has to do with the artist's approach to her work. Is she expressing a culture she has wholeheartedly and honestly embraced, or is she making Navajo-looking jewelry because those items are selling well this year? Is she working from a position of respect for the culture she is representing, or is she working in turquoise and silver because those materials are inexpensive and easy to handle? As folklorist Henry Glassie put it, "Internal authenticity involves artistic expression without irony."[2]

Following those perspectives, Cohn maintains that he is working from a position that is informed by his best understanding of Inuit culture. He was not born and raised in the Arctic, but quite a few Inuit artists have spent their lives in Toronto and Vancouver. If authenticity involves the enthusiastic embrace of a culture, then Cohn insists he is working with Kunuk to create authentic Inuit videos.

I understand and appreciate Cohn's argument.[3] Blood quantum might be a necessary measure for the inclusion or exclusion of individuals in a group entitled to certain benefits, but in the realm of artistic expression, it is the relationship of the artist to the culture revealed in his work — and not the number of generations his family has lived in a region, or the purity of his ancestry, or the color of his skin and hair — that determines whether the work is authentically representative of a culture.

Does this mean that Cohn has "gone native," that he is yet another example of a white man immersing himself in an exotic culture and taking on the trappings of its outward appearance? No. It means that Cohn has gained an understanding of the ways Inuit view the universe, and he finds them persuasive and compelling. He is skeptical of the views embraced by many people in southern Canada, the United States, and Europe. He finds in Inuit culture a greater appreciation for the kinds of human expression that he pursues in his own art. For that reason, he embraces Inuit culture to a great degree, even to the point of being offered — and accepting — an Inuit name.

Cohn's expertise in videography has been invaluable to Isuma. He moved to video when the technology was still young, finding the medium expressive, innovative, and well-suited to the kind of underground, countercultural approach he wanted to take with his art.

Among the perspectives Cohn brings to Isuma is a clear sense of time as a videographic tool. For one of his early video projects, he developed a video exhibition for the White House Conference on Children and Youth. The assignment called for an exploration of childhood development, a way to show viewers how children grow and incorporate new skills and abilities into their worlds. After thinking about how to tackle this assignment, Cohn came up with an idea. He videotaped eight children for a straight thirty minutes each — no camera cuts, no editing, just aiming the camera at the child and keeping the tape running. The children were spaced out according to age: a six-month-old child, a one-year-old, a two-year-old, and so on. To give the exhibition some unity, he had each child begin with eating. Then he followed the child for the next thirty minutes, taping everything the child chose to do.

For the exhibition, he arranged eight screens in a semicircle and played the videos simultaneously. At the start of each cycle, visitors to the show could see the entire array of children eating — the youngest being fed by his mother, the one-year-old stuffing cereal into his mouth with his hands, the two-year-old using a spoon, and so on. Then the activities diverged as the children pursued their own inclinations, each videotape showing the kinds of things the child could do and was interested in. When the videos ended, there was a pause for reflection and discussion, and then they began again.

That kind of loose directing, allowing the subjects to choose their actions and reactions, remains a hallmark of Cohn's work. Much of the production and camera work he does for Isuma involves creating a scene — hunting caribou in the Arctic in the 1930s, for example — and then turning the actors loose with just a general idea of what they are supposed to do. That kind of spontaneity gives many of the Isuma videos a sense of grounded realism. It also allows the actors, almost all of whom have no professional acting experience, the chance to simply be themselves and carry out the mission at hand. For most of the videos, the actors do not have to memorize long scripts or try to adopt new personae. They simply understand the situation and what they are supposed to do, then they go out and do it. They say whatever they want to say — just as people in those situations would — and they pursue the task Cohn gives them with a reliance on their training and experiences. *The Fast Runner* is an exception to this approach, as is Isuma's second major film, *The Journals of Knud Rasmussen*. For these films, Kunuk and Cohn issued scripts and worked with the actors to develop characters and to follow a preplanned story arc.

Cohn also handles many of the business aspects of the Isuma enterprise. He spends much of his time applying for grants, following up on grant applications, and managing the grant money. He makes sure the actors and other contributors are paid, and he juggles the finances when things get tight.

Pauloosie Qulitalik

Pauloosie Qulitalik has appeared in several Isuma videos, and in some non-Isuma movies as well. Qulitalik was born in Argo Bay, a small Inuit community far to the west of Igloolik. (Argo Bay is in the Northwest Territories, outside the region that split off to form Nunavut.) He moved to the Igloolik area when he was adopted by his grandmother. One of Igloolik's prominent elders and chair of the Igloolik School Committee at the time of filming of *The Fast Runner*, he plays an important role in the culture of Igloolik. He speaks primarily in Inuktitut, and he carries with him a great deal of traditional Inuit knowledge. One snowy morning during the filming of *The Fast Runner*, Qulitalik was working just outside the large sod house that had been built for the set. He was calmly building a small igloo by himself, puffing on his short pipe while expertly fitting the blocks together.

Qulitalik's first major film credit is *White Dawn*, the 1974 adaptation of the novel by James Houston. Qulitalik signed on with the film as a small-part actor and to build igloos and other parts of the set. *White Dawn* shows the story of three whalers who find themselves living among the Netsilik Eskimos when their ship is trapped in the ice.

In Igloolik, Qulitalik pursued his interest in video and film work by signing on at the IBC production center in town. He became one of the four founding members of Isuma and acted in the group's

Qaggiq and *Nunaqpa* videos. He also undertook a wide range of roles in the Nunavut series and in subsequent Isuma projects.

Qulitalik takes seriously the role of cultural ambassador for Inuit. He has seen enormous changes in the Arctic during his lifetime — going from life on the land in the traditional, nomadic way to life in town in pre-fab houses with television and the Internet — and he understands the importance of keeping the old knowledge alive.

Paul Apak

The other founding member of Isuma was Paul Apak Angilirq, who died in 1998. Apak originally worked for the IBC office in Igloolik, where he made numerous videos for airing on the network.

He made some independent videos as well. His first major video involved a recreation of the Qitdlarssuaq migration from the Igloolik area to Greenland. As mentioned in chapter one, in the mid-1800s, a shaman named Qitlaq and about forty Inuit migrated from the Igloolik area to northern Greenland in an effort to escape the wrath of a powerful shaman. When he arrived in Greenland and founded his new camp, Qitlaq was dubbed "the Great Qitlaq," or *Qitdlarssuaq*, in Greenlandic.

In an interview with Nancy Wachowich, a professor of anthropology at the University of Aberdeen in Scotland, Apak described how he had grown interested in traditional Inuit culture through his work with the IBC, an interesting example of a new medium sparking interest in an old and deep-rooted culture (Wachowich 2002). He also was driving a dog team at the time, so in 1987, when he heard that a recreation of the Qitdlarssuaq journey was under way, he decided to get involved. He drove his own dog team, and he filmed the entire event. Ultimately, he created a five-part series about the expedition that was aired on IBC.

Apak took part in another journey that resulted in a film project as well. In 1990, he heard about an attempt to cross from Siberia to Alaska in open walrus-skin boats. He was asked if he wanted to join this expedition. He agreed to participate right away, and he filmed that journey for a two-part series for the IBC called *Umiaq*. (*Umiaq* means "women's boat." It refers to the larger boat used for hauling gear, as opposed to the smaller and faster *qajaq* [kayak] used for hunting marine mammals.)

An important component of Apak's work is the close involvement of Inuit elders. Inuktitut has changed over the years, and the proper behavior around various relatives and elders has changed as well. In the interest of authenticity, Apak wanted to make sure that none of his films, including *The Fast Runner*, had characters who violated respectful address, used words or linguistic structures that were not common at the time the scene took place, and so on.

"It is working to preserve both the knowledge and the traditions," he said in the interview with Wachowich. "We try to go back as far as possible with the language, using the old language. So the thing about learning the culture is what makes this film go really far beyond what we expected. We really preserve a lot of things that we wouldn't be able to get at if it wasn't for this legend, this screenplay. We go to the elders and ask information about the old ways, about religion, things that a lot of people don't have an idea of now."

The Birth of Isuma

The Fast Runner, of course, did not emerge from a vacuum. The Isuma producers had first honed their skills through a series of video projects, gaining confidence, experience, and a sense of mission along the way.

The formation of Isuma began when Apak left the IBC, and Kunuk considered following suit. Kunuk had been chafing under the direction he was receiving from IBC headquarters in Ottawa. He objected to the tight budgets and the need to ask permission before buying equipment and other items that his crew needed. When Apak left the corporation over similar frustrations, Kunuk ultimately decided to do the same. Kunuk then talked with Apak about forming their own video organization. They met also with Qulitalik, and they invited Norman Cohn to join them as well. The four producers eventually formed Igloolik Isuma Productions.

The first video Kunuk made after leaving the IBC was *Qaggiq*. (*Qaggiq* refers to a large igloo built for the gathering of several families. The people get together for celebration and companionship.) Shot even before Igloolik Isuma Productions was officially incorporated, *Qaggiq* shows the coming together of several families for fun, food, games, and songs. The film has a small plotline running through it. A young man is thinking about taking a woman as his wife. His parents are eager to see him get married, and the woman's mother is happy about the potential marriage as well. But the woman's father is caught off guard; he hadn't thought it all through. He objects at first, not sure how to react. But his wife works on him a bit, and eventually, during the drum dance celebration inside the large communal igloo, the young man makes his stand. He stares directly at his girlfriend's father and then grabs the young woman's arm. He ushers her out of the igloo, and his declaration is clear: If you're going to stop me, do so now.

The father, caught off guard again, responds with a resigned shrug and sings an ad-libbed *ajaja* song—a loose, often improvised song about whatever is on the singer's mind, usually to the accompaniment of a booming drum—about how the marriage is OK with him now that he's thought it over.

As with all Isuma videos, much of the richness comes from the demonstrations of traditional Inuit lifeways. *Qaggiq*, set in the 1930s, recreates Inuit life in the period after contact with Europeans but before the wholesale changes in Inuit culture brought on by the arrival of outsiders. One scene, for example, shows the building of an igloo, the large one that will be used for the multifamily gathering. The older men scout the snow drifts, probing with a rod to find snow that is packed to the proper density. Then, once the elders have indicated the best sources for igloo snow, the younger men begin to carve blocks and lift them out of the hole. There is something of a competitive air to the process: each of the young men wants to be sure to do well and carry his own weight. Gradually, the igloo takes shape, the older men making adjustments with snow knives while the women and children pack snow into the open cracks between blocks.

The video also demonstrates drum dancing and ajaja singing. For the drum dancing, the men hold the large drum — a skin stretched tight on a wooden frame, with a single handle sticking out — and strike the rim with a mallet, turning the drum to hit opposite edges. The drum gives off a low, steady tone, and the drummer sways to the beat, bent slightly forward and shuffling his feet somewhat. The drum dancer sometimes sings along to his own drumming, but often one or more of the spectators sing instead.

Drum dancing is hard work — the drum is heavy, and shoulder muscles begin to ache quickly — and part of the challenge is to maintain an even rhythm for a long time. Once a drum dancer has had enough, he stops and hands the drum to someone else. That person then begins a beat of his own and performs for the audience.

The drum dancing is typically accompanied by ajaja (also spelled *ayaya*, pronounced a-YAH-yah) singing. Ajaja songs are loose verses that may or may not follow any particular theme. They are broken up with rhythmic chanting, the "ayaya" sounds, and they are often made up on the fly. The songs typically reflect the mood or state of mind of the singer, who might use the song to tell about interesting or unusual things that happened recently, her relationships with other members of the group, etc.

Nunaqpa

The next video Kunuk made — now officially under the Isuma banner — was *Nunaqpa*, which was released in 1991. This video follows a small group of families that are going off to hunt caribou. (*Nunaqpa* means "going inland.") This video is more fully situational, dropping the plotline in favor of a more documentary approach, and the actors were free to work without scripted lines. Instead, they were taught by elders, who showed them how caribou were hunted in the 1930s. They then went onto the land to enact what they had learned.

In the film, the families first make a base camp, where the women and children will stay and wait with the men who are too old to hunt. Then the smaller group of hunters continues into the hills of Baffin Island, searching for caribou. When they find some, they unsheathe their rifles and fire, catching two animals. They butcher the caribou where they fell, caching some of the meat and putting the rest of it into the skins for the trip back to the base camp. The hunters eat, get some rest, and then return to their waiting relatives, who are thrilled to see a successful outcome.

Like *Qaggiq*, *Nunaqpa* offers rich glimpses into traditional Inuit life. When the group is whole, everyone carries something that is essential for their survival and comfort. The packs, made of caribou hide, have single straps that run horizontally across the shoulders, instead of the twin vertical straps used in the South. And sometimes a heavy load is steadied with the aid of a forehead strap.

The hunting party, however, carries far less. They anticipate getting some caribou, so they don't haul much food. And they don't plan to stay out for more than a few days at the most, so they don't need extensive shelters. (The weather at this time of year is cool but not cold.)

One of the most revealing scenes involves the butchering of the caribou. Displaying an intimate knowledge of caribou anatomy, the hunters use small, sharp knives to remove the hide, take out the entrails, cut up the meat, and repackage it all for caching or carrying. The butchering is quick, clean, and orderly; the hide peels off in one piece like a bandage, and the carcass bleeds very little. The hunters clearly have been trained well, and they have skinned caribou often in their real lives.

Saputi

After *Nunaqpa* showed people traditional ways of camping and hunting caribou, Kunuk wanted to create a video about fishing for delicious Arctic char. One of the traditional ways Inuit would catch Arctic char involved building a stone weir, or *saputi*. When the fish tried to migrate past a certain point, Inuit hunters would build a loose stone dam across a large river. The fish would swim that far but be unable to get past the dam. They would swim around the pool, looking for a way through, and were easy to catch.

For the making of *Saputi*, Kunuk followed the same approach he had taken with *Nunaqpa*. He talked with elders about how the weirs were made, what time of year was best, and so on. He also had Qulitalik and other elders involved with the project directly, offering advice and guidance to aid in authenticity. Then, once the actors understood how things were to be done, they were turned loose without any scripted lines. Their job was to do what the elders did: find a good spot at the right time of year, build a stone weir, and harvest the fish.

Unfortunately for the filming of this video, the fish didn't show up. (As Kunuk explained it to me, "The Fish Union didn't cooperate.") The river was flowing, the weir was built, and nothing was happening. In a Hollywood movie the scene would have been declared a failure and another shoot scheduled. But Kunuk understands that Inuit enterprises are highly dependent on the weather, the animals being hunted, and other variables beyond human control. So he continued to make his video even in the absence of fish. Instead of focusing on the harvesting of char, the video became about how people pass the time while waiting for nature to cooperate with their plans. The waiting becomes tedious, and people's minds begin to wander. Imaginations create and distort reality. The spirit world looms close. In the video, one person imagines he can jump across the entire river, a superhuman feat. A short while later the rocks turn into monsters that scare and harass. The fish never did show up, but, as with all outdoor activities in the Arctic, you have to improvise and be nimble enough to create success when original plans fail.

Nunavut

These three videos, *Qaggiq*, *Nunaqpa*, and *Saputi*, were shown in a variety of venues, including some film festivals. They attracted attention and critical praise for their directness and authenticity, and for their depictions of the beauty of the Arctic and the fascinating intricacies of traditional Inuit life. With that success building Isuma's reputation, Kunuk, Apak, Cohn, and Qulitalik embarked on an ambitious project. They decided to capture many facets of Inuit life in a thirteen-part video series called Nunavut. (*Nunavut* means "our land.")

The first video in the series is *Qimuksiq*, which means "dog team." Set somewhat later than the *Qaggiq–Nunaqpa–Saputi* series, which depicted life in the 1930s, *Qimuksiq* shows what life was like in the Igloolik area in 1945. Although the region had been visited by a succession of whalers, missionaries, and explorers, the traditional Inuit way of life had not yet been radically altered by these contacts. *Qimuksiq* follows one Inuit family in particular as they move about the region, hunt for food, and teach their children how to thrive in the Arctic environment.

In the second video of the series, *Avaja*, the family arrives at the place called Avaja (near Igloolik) to find other families already camped there. The families catch up on news and gossip, and they prepare shelters and hunt for food. It is also at Avaja that the families meet a missionary who tries to convince them to follow Christianity. The Inuit aren't sure how to respond, and several people express concern about how this change will affect their traditions and heritage—a theme echoed in *The Journals of Knud Rasmussen*, Isuma's second major film.

In the third installment of the series, *Qarmaq*, an elder recalls the old Inuit traditions and taboos. (*Qarmaq* means "stone house.") The fourth, *Tugaliaq* (Ice Blocks) shows the Inuit debating possible responses to the world war raging in the South. Some talk of using shamanistic powers to bring an end to the conflict. The fifth, *Angiraq* (Home), shows everyday life in a comfortable, stable Inuit community, complete with the bickering of children.

The sixth, seventh, and eighth kick off 1946, with expanding days and moderating temperatures. *Auriaq* (Stalking) shows the endless hunting that goes on in the spring as depleted stores are replenished and hungry stomachs are filled. *Qulangisi* (Seal Pups) offers a glimpse into the hunt for young seals, an activity in which everyone participates. (Young seals are generally considered to taste better than adults.) *Avamuktalik* (Fish Swimming Back and Forth) focuses on young men fishing with spears.

With the arrival of summer comes the walrus hunt; *Aiviaq* (Walrus) captures this dangerous but rewarding activity. The video also shows the arrival of a priest in the traditional walrus-hunting area—an omen considered dangerous by many of the Inuit. *Qaisut* (Qaisut is a region known for its cliffs) shows a happy time after a successful walrus hunt; a hungry polar bear, however, threatens the camp.

Fall arrives and begins its rapid fade into winter. *Tuktuliaq* (Caribou Hunt) shows the trek to Baffin Island for caribou hunting, a theme similar to that depicted in *Nunaqpa*. In *Unaaq* (Harpoon), the family sits in a stone house and enjoys stories and friendship as the weather cools outside. *Quviasuvik* (Happy Day) shows the odd syncretism that Christmas has become in Inuit life: part Christian, part European, part Inuit, but still involving good food and companionship.

Arvik!

The Nunavut series was greeted enthusiastically by critics and scholars, and it further cemented Isuma's reputation as a first-rate video organization. In the build-up to the creation of *The Fast Runner*, Isuma made a few other videos as well.

One important video from this time is *Arvik!*. Until this video, most of Isuma's work could be categorized as cultural re-creation, drawing authenticity—as Kunuk would emphasize—from the knowledge of elders and not, as in *Nanook of the North*, based on stereotypes common in the South. But *Arvik!*—*arvik* means "bowhead whale"—is more properly a political documentary, an effort to present a particular point of view in clear and direct terms.

The video focuses on the hunting of bowhead whales, which was declared illegal by international treaty in 1966. At the time of the first European excursions into the North American Arctic, bowhead whales were plentiful, despite being hunted by the Inuit for millennia. British, Scottish, and American whaling ships, however, were quick to head to the Baffin region to harvest this large and lucrative animal. (Bowheads were also called "right whales" because, from a financial perspective, they were the "right" whale to hunt.) In a matter of decades, the population of bowheads in the Arctic had been slashed to just a few thousand.

The international ban on bowhead hunting applied to the Inuit as well, however, and suddenly — because of the mismanagement of outside whaling enterprises — the Inuit found themselves forbidden to hunt an animal they had hunted for generations. Not only was a source of food eliminated for the Inuit, but the body of knowledge about bowhead hunting began to disappear as well.

In 1994, an Igloolik elder named Noah Piugattuk addressed the community on the local radio station. He was dying, and said he wanted to taste bowhead blubber, called Muktuk, one last time before he was gone. This call created a significant clash. In traditional Inuit systems, a request made by an elder was serious, and the younger people were expected to fulfill it. But the laws of Canada and the international treaties made the hunting of bowhead illegal. So the people of Igloolik were caught in a cultural bind.

Not long after that, some hunters in a boat came across a bowhead that had been injured. They knew it would die soon, and they were aware of Piugattuk's request, so they killed the whale and brought it to shore. Word spread quickly; the video shows dozens of people on the rocky beach butchering the animal and eating the Muktuk. Noah Piugattuk enjoyed his taste of Muktuk and the respect shown to him by the hunters. He died a few months later.

The video then shifts to the court trial in which the hunters were accused of illegally killing a protected animal. The government presented its case, which was fairly clear because the hunters did not deny killing the bowhead. But then several Inuit leaders made their case, arguing that they lived by a set of laws also — and that the hunters were obeying the law prescribed by Inuit tradition. The hunters were caught between two systems, the argument went, and it would be unfair to punish them for having to choose.

Ultimately, the hunters were acquitted. Even more, the Canadian government agreed to allow the Inuit to hunt one bowhead whale every two years. The first hunt was given to the community of Rankin Inlet.

But the erosion of knowledge during the ban on bowhead hunting had taken its toll. The hunters were not chosen according to traditional means, which would have put the very best bowhead hunters on the job. Instead, it was done by lottery, and few of the hunters involved had the necessary skill to kill a bowhead properly. They found a bowhead, harpooned it to attach floats to it, and then shot it — and it promptly sank to the bottom of the ocean. The hunters tried to find the carcass in a variety of ways, including renting a small submarine unit with a built-in camera, but nothing worked. Days later, after hope was almost gone, the whale floated to the surface. The carcass was too bloated and rotten for the meat to be used for food, but the Muktuk was still good. It was shared with elders from several Inuit communities.

Arvik! makes its point clearly: the ban on bowhead hunting was imposed on the Inuit without consultation and through no fault of the Inuit themselves. Inuit had been hunting bowhead whales for thousands of years without reducing the herd, but European and American whalers had attacked the bowhead population without restraint. Ultimately, the video suggests, listening to the wisdom of the Inuit — in particular, the wisdom of the elders — would have prevented a great deal of hardship.

Since then, Isuma has been producing videos at a fast pace. The biggest achievement since *The Fast Runner* has been the group's second full-length feature, *The Journals of Knud Rasmussen*, which received somewhat cooler reviews from critics than did *The Fast Runner*. But Isuma has made other videos as well, including *Nipi*, *Kunuk Family Reunion*, *Qallunajatut* (Urban Inuk), *Kiviaq Versus Canada*, and others. The Isuma website (www.isuma.ca) offers a complete list of recent projects.

CHAPTER FOUR

Isuma's Motives

Understanding the reasons behind a producer's work is vital to understanding the work itself. Did she create a movie with the goal of making money? Was she trying to advance his own career? Was she trying to make an economic impact in some part of the world? Was she trying to express a set of ideas that she holds dear? Exploring those questions can shed light on the intent behind a movie and the significance that movie might carry.

When Kunuk started making videos in 1981, he was drawn by the images and characters he saw when he watched Hollywood westerns and crime dramas. But Kunuk — and Isuma — are compelled by much more than mimicry or a desire to make a big splash at the box office. As Kunuk asks, "Can Inuit bring storytelling into the new millennium? Can we listen to our elders before they all pass away? Can producing community TV in Igloolik make our community, region and country stronger? Is there room in Canadian filmmaking for our way of seeing ourselves?" (Igloolik Isuma Productions 2002, 15).

Kunuk is driven by more than just a desire to increase the volume of Inuit voices. Information and stories about the Inuit have been created and disseminated for centuries — almost entirely by non-Inuks, who had their own agendas, biases, blind spots, and personal tastes. Some were more serious and professional than others. At the extreme end of the spectrum are movies like *Enuk*, starring Anthony Quinn as an Inuk (he was a Mexican-American actor best known for his portrayal of Zorba the Greek); the movie also featured Hawaiians playing Inuit characters and igloos built out of Styrofoam blocks. Even such ostensibly ethnographic works as *Nanook of the North* present flawed and manipulated information.

In that movie, for example, Nanook is portrayed as a spear hunter, even though he had owned a rifle for years; director Robert Flaherty was trying to make the Inuit seem more primitive and exotic than they were.

Kunuk's motives for making videos about the Inuit include a desire to correct the misperceptions that thrive in the southern world. But they also include a belief that the best people to talk about the Inuit are the Inuit themselves. Additional motives color his work and his efforts as well, including a desire to express his admiration for the people who made life in the Arctic possible.

Appreciation of the Elders

Throughout its videos, Isuma emphasizes the importance of respect for elders and ancestors. *Qaggiq*, *Nunaqpa*, and *Saputi* all focus on the value of elders' insights; Kunuk and Cohn talked with elders at length about how hunting, fishing, igloo building, and other activities were done before Inuit culture collided with European and American approaches and goods. They also learned from elders the ways in which people treated each other, proper forms of address, taboos, and other facets of Inuit culture that shaped everyday behavior. Their mission was to understand the wisdom that the elders possessed and then convey some of that knowledge to the viewers of their videos.

Arvik! and *Nipi* focus even more conspicuously on the value of the elders, shifting from a documentary approach to a more direct way of getting the message across. These videos use clear, straightforward terms to tell viewers that the elders are to be valued for their knowledge, their experience, and their insights.

And, of course, *The Fast Runner* presents elders in a strong and respectful light. At the beginning of the film, Kumaglak, the elder running the camp, is revered, and his word is taken seriously. In proper Inuit fashion, a young person would become an elder through experience, survival, patience, and courage, but Sauri disrupts all that by bringing in the evil shaman who kills Kumaglak.

That act not only removes the camp leader, making way for Sauri's ascension, it also disrupts the traditional systems of authority. Sauri becomes the leader not through his demonstrated wisdom but through his cruelty and cunning. This disruption paves the way for the misery that follows, including Sauri's own murder at the hands of his son, Uqi.

At the film's conclusion, after Atanarjuat has opened the way for healing by refusing to continue the feud, Qulitalik and Panikpak are able to drive off the evil shaman and restore the proper leadership role of the elders. It is with this restored authority that Panikpak is able to banish Uqi, Puja, and their gang from the camp — and the villains leave without putting up a fight. The rule of the elders once again commands respect.

Isuma also honored elders by including them in every stage of the *Fast Runner* project, from scriptwriting to costuming and set design. Herve Paniaq, one of the writers, offered valuable insights into how people would have behaved and how they would have spoken in the old times. Pauloosie Qulitalik, who played the part of Qulitalik in the film but also served as a consultant, igloo builder, and other roles, was on hand continually to correct errors, improve the style of the older form of Inuktitut, and ensure that the architecture, dog-team use, and other aspects of the Inuit lifeways shown in the film were accurate.

In addition, *The Fast Runner* acknowledges the wisdom and courage of the ancestors. Kunuk and the others at Isuma feel a great debt to ancestors, both recent and ancient, who figured out how to live in the harsh Arctic environment, how to function as effective households and teams to ensure survival and comfort, and how to build not just a meager existence but a thriving, joyous life in a forbidding part of the world. By reaching back five hundred years to show the Atanarjuat legend, the Isuma producers were able to demonstrate to viewers — both through highlighted activities and through quiet, background action — the myriad ways in which the ancestors turned a challenging environment into a rich and fulfilling world.

Today, Igloolik is a town of approximately 1,500 people. Some of the town's recent population growth can be traced to the location of some Nunavut territorial government offices there. The community is often considered among the most traditional of the Nunavut towns.

A short distance outside the town of Igloolik lies the rock that Atanarjuat used as a bench. He would sit on this rock and wait for the whales he hunted to wash up on the shore. Today the waterline is hundreds of feet away from the rock because the island has been rising since the departure of the glaciers after the last ice age.

Zacharias Kunuk, in his wolfskin parka, talks with Pauloosie Qulitalik, who is building an igloo for the set of *The Fast Runner*.

Pauloosie Qulitalik builds an igloo on the set of *The Fast Runner*. Qulitalik, an Igloolik elder, has participated in several Isuma videos, in addition to films by other organizations.

Zacharias Kunuk, in the wolfskin parka, shoots footage during a *qaggiq*, a gathering of people for companionship and festivities, in a large ice igloo built in Igloolik in 1999.

Zacharias Kunuk works at the offices of Igloolik Isuma Productions during the filming of *The Fast Runner*.

Zacharias Kunuk, left, works on a project with Norman Cohn, right, in the offices of Igloolik Isuma Productions. In the middle is James Ungalaq, who often contributes to Isuma projects.

Lucy Tulugarjuk poses in front of the former Catholic church in Igloolik, with her daughter Kayla in her amauti hood. Tulugarjuk played the part of Puja, the evil temptress, in *The Fast Runner*.

Sylvia Ivalu, who played Atuat, Atanarjuat's wife, in *The Fast Runner*.

Response

Another important aspect of Isuma's work, including *The Fast Runner*, involves responding to media messages coming from the South. In the early 1920s Robert Flaherty made his historic film *Nanook of the North*, venturing to the Arctic coast of Hudson Bay to record and document myriad facets of Inuit life for southern viewers. The film follows the activities of Nanook, an Inuit hunter, and his family as they go about hunting, house building, and other routine activities in the North.

That film, which launched the documentary genre, is the outcome of an extraordinary effort, and Flaherty deserves a great deal of praise for his vision, his talent, and his determination. (After extensive filming on the coast of Hudson Bay, Flaherty lost all his film in a fire and had to head north all over again to remake the movie.) *Nanook* triggers a much different reaction in Kunuk, however. In Kunuk's estimation, the film established numerous denigrating stereotypes about Inuit and offers a string of insulting depictions of the Inuit and their abilities. The scene that infuriates Kunuk the most shows Flaherty playing a phonograph for Nanook. Nanook appears to be stupefied by the sound coming from the machine, and in his wonder over this marvelous device, he picks up a phonograph record and bites it. Kunuk is horrified that this scene makes Inuit appear to be dimwitted simpletons who can't tell the difference between a man-made device and food.

Part of Isuma's mission is to present Inuit life to viewers without the mistakes, stereotypes, and insults that find their way into southern depictions of the Arctic. Kunuk and the other producers see Isuma's videos as a chance to correct misperceptions by showing that with the right knowledge and understanding — as well as the right attitude and patience — people can live well in the Arctic. Inuit aren't backward and simple, Kunuk argues, but rather brilliant and inventive. He marvels at the design of the igloo and the simple effectiveness of the dogsled. The ancestors who developed those technologies were clearly geniuses, he said to me, and *The*

Fast Runner and the other Isuma products serve as testimonials to that fact. As Paul Apak put it,

> There are a number of differences between what we are doing and other movies that have been produced regarding our Inuit culture. This movie will be based on an Inuit legend and also it is all going to be in Inuktitut, in the first place. And also, all of the actors will have to be Inuk. No Japanese or whoever who pretend to be Inuit. You know. It will be done the Inuit way. We want it to be like the way things happened in real life. That is what we are going to do. (Igloolik Isuma Productions 2002, 21)

Priorities

This Inuit approach to videography extends beyond the video products to the processes themselves. As Sally Berger wrote in an articulate and artfully considered essay published in *Felix* in 1995, "The process of making these videotapes provides the primary reason and meaning for their creation" (Berger 1995, 109). Among the reasons that Kunuk and Apak left the IBC was that they did not like the southern approach to work that the IBC has adopted. At the IBC, the workday has boundaries, as it typically does in southern Canada and elsewhere. Employees are expected to show up at a particular time and work until another designated moment on the clock. They get time off for breaks and lunch, but otherwise they are supposed to be on the job and working hard.

That ethic might make sense in southern and urban settings, but Kunuk finds it at odds with Inuit rhythms. He is anything but lazy — his list of videos, awards, and other accomplishments speaks to his productivity and abilities — but he does not want to subordinate the rest of his life to his workday. He told me once that if a polar bear shows up near Igloolik, people should be free to drop what they're doing and go after it. In traditional Inuit life, that would not only be possible, it would be expected. But in the southern system of working, you have to stay on the job until the clock says you can leave. If the weather is beautiful and the fishing is good, Kunuk feels, people should go to the bays and get fish. If the weather is terrible and traveling outside is miserable or dangerous, people should be free to stay home. The clock should not dictate the priorities of the day.

At Isuma, Kunuk and the others follow a much more traditionally Inuit way of working. They show up when they are ready and they work when they can. Making sure you're on the job from one specified time to another is a Qallunaat way of working, not an Inuit way, and Isuma runs on Inuit rhythms as much as possible.

Other Inuit approaches hold at Isuma as well. Ironically, in a criticism put forth in an article published in FUSE, film studies professor Laura U. Marks argues that Kunuk is positioned too fully in an *auteur* role, using a concept first put forth by François Truffaut in 1954 (Marks 1998). She argues that Kunuk is often given sole credit for Isuma's successes and productions, as though the other people of Isuma and the environment and infrastructure that made those triumphs possible do not exist. She points quite rightly to the collaborative nature of both filmmaking and Inuit culture in her argument, but she offers little support for her contention that credit is heaped on Kunuk alone, operating largely from a perspective that ascribes an auteurist reading of all film enterprises to typical and widespread southern audiences and critics. She also offers no direct research whatsoever in the article: no original quotes from Kunuk, Cohn, or the other producers, or from people in Igloolik, or even from critics and film scholars. All the research in the piece stemmed from secondary sources. This article was published while I was in Igloolik working with Isuma, and the reaction there was a mixture of disappointment and frustration. Had Marks talked to Kunuk, she could have more forcefully made the point that any auteur status conferred on him was the result of southern assumptions and runs counter to Kunuk's own desire to emphasize the importance of collaboration in Inuit culture and in Isuma's operations. In response to urgings from Kunuk and Cohn, I wrote an article for the same publication that endeavored to offer a more grounded view (Evans 2000).

Just as he argues for Inuit approaches to work, time, and team-work, Kunuk laments the recent emphasis on private property that has come to Igloolik. Not long ago, he says, if you saw a whale in the bay you could just grab any boat on the beach and go after it. Now you have to have permission in advance or risk being arrested for theft. Isuma operates on a more relaxed system of property own-ership. One time, when I was interviewing Kunuk before heading out to a rehearsal of some scenes for *The Fast Runner*, I looked out the window and saw that my snowmobile was gone. A while later it was back. I don't know who took it or why, but at Isuma, people feel free to use whatever is available without worrying about who owns it.

Industrial Component

The vast majority of Inuit in Igloolik survive on government sub-sidies and hunting. With the exception of government positions, municipal service jobs, and a few hourly openings at the local stores, there are very few opportunities to earn money. Most of the housing is provided through government programs, and the Hunters and Trappers Organization administers a program that provides boats, snowmobiles, and other gear essential for catching food. But some goods require cash, and most of a family's government subsidies go toward food, clothing, and other basic necessities.

This situation locks Igloolik into a "company store" kind of sys-tem. Families buy supplies at the store on credit, then pay off that debt when the government check comes in. Because almost nothing is left over once the bills have been paid, no money is available for saving, investment, or growth. This cash-based economy forcibly displaced the subsistence economy that had flourished in the Arctic for centuries, but not enough jobs are available to allow people in Igloolik to succeed financially.

Moviemaking, however, can and does bring in substantial amounts of cash to Isuma, and through Isuma to the rest of the Igloolik economy. Cohn calls this aspect of videography the "indus-trial component." During the filming of *The Fast Runner*, Isuma employed dozens of people as actors, costumers, set designers, dog-team wranglers, and even caterers and drivers. When funds came in from granting agencies, the employees were paid, and they then could buy the things their families needed. The money went back into the Igloolik economy, to the stores, to the Hunters and Trappers Organization, and to other places where goods could be purchased. People were able to fix up their homes, buy new clothes, and purchase other items that improved their lives.

Ironically, television is often blamed for inflating people's desires for goods, but in Igloolik it is the making of videos — many of which are shown on television through Isuma's own local channel, the IBC, APTN, and other venues — that brings in the cash necessary to fulfill those desires. The people of Igloolik are as entitled as anyone else to nice clothing, iPods, and anything else they choose to buy. Through Isuma's ability to attract cash, people working with Kunuk and Cohn receive funds that allow them to buy what they want.

The funds from granting agencies, however, do not flow smoothly. Cohn works hard to forge relationships with granting organizations, understand the requirements and application procedures, and submit materials designed to bring in the funds necessary to make videos. When a check arrives, the cash flows to people who have put time and effort into the video projects. When that money is gone and some time will elapse before the next influx of cash, the people working on the projects must sometimes wait patiently for their next paycheck.

During the filming of *The Fast Runner*, for example, some grant money that Cohn felt had been promised to Isuma did not arrive. The granting agency had already emptied its budget for the year, and no additional funds were available for it to disburse until the next funding cycle. Isuma had no choice but to suspend filming, pack up the costumes and the sets into large metal shipping containers, and wait until the money came in. People who were owed money were offered shares in the film; they could use the shares to collect their pay when the next grant check came in, and the shares were also good for a percentage of the film's future profits. In this way,

Isuma was able to bridge the gap between checks and keep every-one focused on making *The Fast Runner*. Ultimately, more money did come through, but not before so much time had elapsed that continuity became of concern. Had any of the actors grown taller, cut their hair short, gained or lost weight? When filming finally resumed, Kunuk and Cohn realized they had to discard all their previous footage and start from scratch. They took advantage of the fresh start to make some changes in the film, including bringing in a new actor to play Atanarjuat. Nataar Ungalaaq, who had been assigned a smaller role, became the new male lead.

Inuktitut

Another goal that Isuma values is the preservation — and even the improvement — of the Inuktitut language. Inuktitut is a grammati-cally regular language that is highly flexible. Words are broken in the middle for the addition of modifiers; in addition to adding a suffix or prefix, as is done in English, speakers of Inuktitut insert "chunks" into the middle of words to modify the meaning.

Inuktitut also has syllables that carry meaning in ways that are not found in English. For example, *nuliaq* means "wife." If I wanted to specify that I was talking about the woman I married, as opposed to someone else's wife, I would have to add a word in English: "my wife." In Inuktitut, I would add a syllable that indicates possession. The syllable that indicates "mine" is-*ga*, and when it is added as a suffix to a word ending in *q*, the *g* is dropped and the *q* is changed to an *r*: *nuliaq* becomes *nuliara*.[1] The word for "love" is *nagligi-*, with some kind of ending required. Inuktitut has endings that mean "I→you," "I→her," "he→me," etc. So I would add the ending that means "I→her" to nagligi- to create *nagligiara*. Ultimately, then, *nuliara nagligiara* literally means "Wife (mine) love I her." Of course, that comes across as "I love my wife."

This flexibility and precision allow some ideas to be expressed in Inuktitut that are difficult to say in English. For that reason — and for reasons of culture, history, and respect — many people in the Arctic are interested in preserving Inuktitut as a thriving and modern language. In fact, the government of Nunavut at its founding declared that Inuktitut would be the language in which governmental business would be done; the legislators took that step in an effort to maintain a vital role for Inuktitut in the Arctic.

The Isuma producers, like the producers at the IBC, are also interested in preserving Inuktitut, and that is why Inuktitut is the language used in all Isuma videos. In fact, when Zacharias Kunuk accepted the Camera d'Or Award at the Cannes Film Festival, he delivered his acceptance speech entirely in Inuktitut, just to make the point that the language is alive and active.

Also, by reaching back through time and setting their videos in the distant past, Kunuk and the others at Isuma can create opportunities for young actors to learn the old forms of Inuktitut from the elders. Many of the people speaking Inuktitut today acknowledge that they are using a "baby talk" version of the language, and that the older Inuktitut was much richer and more colorful. The actors in *The Fast Runner* had to spend hours learning how to speak the more ancient form of Inuktitut from elders who still had a command of it.

Representation

Another goal held by the Isuma producers has to do with the presentation of Inuit values to the rest of the world. Kunuk and the others knew that *The Fast Runner* would be seen by a wide audience in the South, and they wanted to deliver a message to that audience about the perspectives held by the Inuit. Included in these perspectives are a level of respect that southern peoples often find either quaint or refreshing, a way of interacting with the natural world that ensures sustainability and prosperity, and an approach to interpersonal relations that is more relaxed and less inhibited by religious mores common in the South. Part of the *Fast Runner*'s message is an uplifting moral that required the producers to change the standard ending to the legend of Atanarjuat.

In the versions of the legend described in chapter five and in other variants circulating in the Arctic, the Atanarjuat story does not end with the hero deciding against revenge. In the oral versions of the legend, Atanarjuat comes back to the camp in Igloolik and prepares a meal in a slippery igloo for his rivals. He then kills Uqi and the others and either kills or enslaves their families. The narrative circle is complete through the settling of the score: your family attacked my family, now I'm attacking you.

Despite such book titles as *Never in Anger*, the Inuit were (and are) capable of murder when the necessary circumstances arose. In a wonderful book about the Inuit titled *People from Our Side*, Peter Pitseolak tells of a whaling crew that was treating the local Inuit badly. The Inuit put up with the abuse for as long as they could, then decided to get rid of the offensive whalers. The Inuit made each whaler a special gift of sealskin mittens and presented the mittens to the whalers one night. The whalers put the mittens on, and the Inuit helped them lace them up. But the mittens had no separate extension for the thumb; they were basically pouches that tied on at the wrist. Once the whalers were wearing their new gifts, the Inuit pulled out knives and began to stab them to death. Without the use of their thumbs and fingers, the whalers were unable to use their rifles, and they all perished (Pitseolak and Eber 1975, 22–23).

But the people of Isuma wanted to deliver a different message to the world, a message having more to do with harmony, respect, and restraint than with anger and revenge. So, for the movie, they changed the ending of the legend to reflect that message. They chose to emphasize balance and selflessness over ego and ambition.

Several critics noticed the uplifting ending and observed that it did not reflect the typical way such legends ended. Some of the critics understood the intent of the screenwriters and responded accordingly. Others, however, missed the point rather badly. One such critic, Justin Shubow, writing for the website published by *The American Prospect*, called the ending a "misrepresentation" and argued that "at the film's core is a crucial lie." He positioned the legend as somehow unaltered from its original form, as if stories from oral literature existed in some perfect state and are corrupted over time. And having done so, he decried the ending shown in the film, which he called a "surprisingly pacifist turn." Drawing on his knowledge of "some basic world myths," he found it difficult to believe that anything other than a violent, vengeance-filled ending would be authentic.

To investigate his suspicion that the ending had been changed, he contacted Isuma. Both Cohn and Kunuk acknowledged that they had written an ending that deviates from that found in most of the oral versions of the legend. Kunuk offered this explanation, quoted in Shubow's critique: "Every generation has their version. It was a message more fitting for our times. Killing people doesn't solve anything."

Fueled with this proof that some kind of misrepresentation had occurred, Shubow noted that while screenwriters often employ their own creative license in adapting oral literature to film, this particular film "was intended as an indelible document to preserve an oral tradition — and as such, it presents itself as painstakingly authentic." He cited the use of the elders to ensure the film's cultural accuracy as evidence that "The Fast Runner" was billed as somehow unchanged in the transition from oral to filmic form. He went on to condemn the film as "profoundly misleading" because he detected an implication that mercy colored the ending of the "original myth." He tossed in such terms as "whitewash" and "veneer of contemporary morality," arguing that the change amounted to misrepresentation because "most moviegoers were never the wiser" (Shubow 2003).

Shubow, who was a graduate student in philosophy at the University of Michigan at the time he wrote that review, missed several key points. For example, in addition to his mislabeling of the Atanarjuat story as a myth (it is a legend) and getting the time frame wrong (it is set five hundred years ago, not a thousand, as he claims) he seems to ignore the very explanation that Kunuk gave him. Kunuk explained that every generation has its version of the legend, and that insight reflects a sophisticated understanding of the nature of oral literature. As folklorists have understood for decades, stories change as they are passed along, and those changes speak to the needs, views, and concerns of the people doing the telling. If a story has outlived its message, people stop telling it. But if the message is modified to suit current perspectives, then people continue to tell it. It is not wrong or misleading to alter a story. In fact, that alteration is exactly what gives the story currency in an ever-changing world.

As any good storyteller knows, stories have to be adjusted to suit the audience. In *The Singer of Tales*, Albert Lord noted that Slavic ballad singers were adept at shortening their songs as needed to suit the mood of the listeners. If the listeners were content and engaged, the singer would stick to the long version. But as soon as they showed signs of restlessness or boredom, the singer would begin to cut out certain sections of the ballad to reach the ending sooner (Lord 1971). A finely tuned understanding of the audience is the key to successful storytelling — and to successful moviemaking. Kunuk and Cohn understood what their audience would want in the story they were telling, and the critical acclaim and extensive awards showered on the movie suggest that their understanding was on target. As the movie makes clear, the story was *based* on an Inuit legend. Kunuk and Cohn modified the story line to suit audience expectations, just as any good storyteller would do. Nowhere do the producers claim that the film shows the legend exactly as it is told in the Arctic. In fact, such a claim would be ludicrous; as I discuss in chapter five, there are numerous versions of the legend, and these versions necessarily diverge from each other in key ways. No single variant offers the "official" version of the story.

Shubow tries to position the changed ending as a kind of fraud, but that position reveals a serious misunderstanding of the nature of authenticity. In this case, *The Fast Runner* is offered as an authentic representation of Inuit culture and lifeways, not a clone of a piece of oral literature. The accuracy lies in the ways that the characters go about their lives — their clothing, their architecture, their language, their games and pastimes, their interactions with each other — not in the unaltered presentation of a story line. Shubow notes that the film's press kit states that elders assisted in the project to ensure cultural accuracy. He points to that statement as support for his claim that the producers should have known better than to violate the legend's plot. What Shubow fails to grasp, however, is that the elders were included because Kunuk and Cohn wanted to make sure that the actions, interactions, and lifeways exhibited by the characters came across in ways that meshed with the elders' understanding of Inuit life at that time. None of the elders I interviewed formally and informally during my nine-month stay in Igloolik complained about the updated ending, evidence of the flexibility of folklore.

I will offer one last point in response to Shubow. As the versions discussed later in this book demonstrate, the movie actually offers numerous changes to the versions of the legend in current circulation. The rationale for the feud, for example, is different: in one variant, it is the brothers' superior hunting skills; in another, it is their haughty attitude. In the movie, it is the introduction of evil by an ambitious son, coupled with the machinations of Puja (who is not mentioned in the collected versions at all). The oral versions do not have many of the characters who appear in the movie, including Qulitalik, Panikpak, and other major figures. These characters were added to make a successful transition from oral legend to film.

To underscore his assertion that a peaceful ending is fraudulent, Shubow insists that the Inuit were "without laws, police, or prisons," a position that exposes a southern view of social control; in Inuit society, the power of the elders to resolve disputes was potent and respected. Shubow continues that narrowly southern perspective when he assaults the film as misleading, even though it "presents itself as painstakingly authentic" (Shubow 2003). The triumph of the film lies in its highly authentic presentation of Inuit life before contact with Europeans, and the change in the story line reflects an insightful appreciation of the demands of modern film audiences.

Art

Kunuk's success as a filmmaker sometimes overshadows his impressive career as a carver. Like many people in the Arctic, he carves soapstone and other materials into beautiful depictions of Inuit life and thinking. When he made the transition to film, he found a familiar medium in many ways. He can shape the images to suit his vision. He can juxtapose scenes to create harmonics of meaning. And he can work with physical materials — actors, costumes, sets, props, cameras, lights — to build a communication with the world that transcends the physical.

He also found a medium that is more flexible and forgiving than stone. He explained to me once that if you break off a piece of the sculpture you're making, you have to change the plan: "turns out that hunter didn't have a spear after all." In film, you can shoot and reshoot until the product on the screen reflects the vision in your mind.

Kunuk uses his videographic art for a wide range of motives: to express his respect for elders and ancestors; to counteract the misleading or misguided depictions of the Inuit offered by southern filmmakers, explorers, and missionaries; to reclaim for the Inuit some of the right to tell their own stories; to demonstrate the viability of an Inuit approach to the working world; to bring a valuable livelihood to many people in Igloolik; to keep the Inuktitut language alive; to share Inuit values and thoughts with the rest of the world. Those motives drew him to film in the first place, with his work at the IBC and his early videos, and they continue to shape his vision through *The Fast Runner* and *The Journals of Knud Rasmussen*. Knowing what his motives and values are sheds a great deal of light on the layers of meaning presented in his films.

CHAPTER FIVE

The Legend and Its Variants

In the late 1990s, Paul Apak Angilirq came up with the idea of turning the legend of Atanarjuat into a full-length feature film that would rely almost entirely on Inuit talent. He collected eight variants of the legend from Igloolik elders, wrote an overarching version of the story in English (which was required for the funding applications), then showed it to the other principals of Igloolik Isuma Productions, the video organization for which he worked. Later drafts of the screenplay were written in Inuktitut by Apak, Norman Cohn, Zacharias Kunuk, Hervé Paniaq, and Pauloosie Qulitalik, working as a team. The final screenplay, completed on March 29, 1998, was also translated into English.

Legends, like any form of oral literature, grow and change over time to reflect the interests of the people telling them. This evolution results in the existence of numerous versions, or "variants," of the story, all in circulation at the same time, with no one variant serving as the "official" or "real" version. Even when a variant is frozen in film or ink, it remains just one of numerous extant versions.

Folklorists, anthropologists, and other scholars often collect and study the various versions of a story to discern differences that can shed light on the culture in question. Because *The Fast Runner* represents just one version of the many in existence telling the Atanarjuat story, exploring the ways in which it echoes or contradicts other versions can illuminate the goals of the producers and the texture of Inuit culture.

The Film Version

The version of the legend told in the film embraces many characters, but at its center is Atanarjuat. Atanarjuat's family — including his father, Tulimaq; his mother, Pitaaluk; and his older brother, Aamarjuaq — belongs to a small band of Inuit living in the Igloolik area. When Atanarjuat is just six months old, a pivotal battle between good and evil takes place in the camp. The camp's leader, Kumaglak, has made the small band of families prosperous and healthy. His success, however, breeds envy; his son thirsts for power and plots to kill him and take over as leader of the camp. The son, Sauri, invites an evil shaman named Tuurngarjuaq to the camp for a duel to the death with his father.

After a fierce battle bridging the physical and spiritual worlds, the evil shaman prevails, and Kumaglak dies. The evil Tuurngarjuaq anoints Sauri the new leader of the group, but this affront to the natural order brings chaos and despair to the band of families. Because of Atanarjuat's popularity and his skill as a hunter, his family in particular suffers scorn and harassment from Sauri and his kin; their food is stolen, their efforts at hunting are disrupted, and their role in the group's activities and decision making is increasingly marginalized.

The film leaps ahead twenty years. Atanarjuat is now a young man whose skill as a hunter has improved his family's situation somewhat. The rest of the camp still treats Atanarjuat and his family as outcasts, giving them only meager portions of the communal hunts and forcing them to pitch their tents some distance away from the others, but on the whole, the family is faring well. Sauri's family, however, continues to act with arrogance and cruelty. Sauri's son, Uqi, becomes Atanarjuat's rival and wastes no opportunity to belittle and frustrate him. Traveling with a small gang of followers, Uqi steals the food that Atanarjuat hunts and commandeers his dogsleds whenever he can.

Uqi's jealousy has at least some rational basis. A beautiful young woman, Atuat, has been promised to Uqi, but she shows increasing fondness for the kinder and more skilled Atanarjuat. Whenever they get a chance, the two young lovers flirt and play games together, and Uqi grows increasingly furious. He challenges Atanarjuat to fights and often complains that Atanarjuat is thwarting his plans. After one hunt, during which Uqi struggles to keep up with Atanarjuat's brother, Aamarjuaq, Uqi's anger boils over. At first Uqi takes his fury out on one of his dogs, but when Aamarjuaq teases him in public, he responds with a threat: "Are you making fun of me? If you think . . . ! If you think you're a better man than me, I . . . ! I could . . . kill you!"[1]

A short while later, Atanarjuat arrives with a sled full of meat, and his father pretentiously declares that a qaggiq — a celebratory gathering in a large igloo — should be held as a way of sharing the food and playing games. The two rival families clearly consider the contests a chance to show up the other, and they go off to prepare.

When the celebration begins, tensions are high in the communal igloo. The space is crowded, and people bump each other and shuffle around for position. The divisions in the camp are clear: Uqi and his family sit on one side, Atanarjuat and his family sit on the other. Some songs are sung to the beat of the large skin drum, and Atuat and another young woman, Puja, compete in a throat-singing contest. Soon, however, Uqi's family sings a song designed to humiliate Atanarjuat. Uqi ends the song by sticking his tongue out at Atanarjuat while his friends laugh. But then it is the other family's turn. Aamarjuaq and his wife, Ulluriaq, sing a song while Atanarjuat beats the drum:

> Aiiiya yaya aiiya ya ya
> Who blames his dog for his empty sled?
> Who blames his father for his empty head?
> Who blames his friends for his empty bed?
> I am Uqi! Uqi! Uqi! Your leader.
> Aiiiya yaya aiiya ya ya, . . . ya ya

When the song is finished, Atanarjuat points his drumstick right at Uqi and farts loudly. Uqi leaps up to fight, but he is restrained by the others around him. Then Sauri declares it is time for the two rivals to square off in a physical contest, with the right to marry Atuat clearly at stake. The game is head punching: Atanarjuat and Uqi will take turns punching each other on the head until one is no longer able to continue. The two men exchange blows until at last Uqi lies dazed on the floor.

Sauri is stunned and refuses to acknowledge that his son has lost the contest. "I'm in charge here! Atuat is already promised to us!" he shouts. Atuat is frozen with fear. She wants to claim Atanarjuat as her husband, but she is afraid to defy Sauri. Finally Panikpak, Uqi's grandmother (and the widow of the murdered camp leader Kumaglak), settles the matter quietly: "My grandson Uqi gave Atuat away . . . by his own choice." Atuat is now free to marry Atanarjuat, but the anger emanating from the rival camp is a clear sign that the troubles will continue.

Five years later, Atanarjuat and his brother are living with their wives in peace. They have food and a nice camp active with members of the family, including Atanarjuat's son, Kumaglak. Atuat is pregnant with their second child, so she has to stay behind while Atanarjuat goes off to hunt caribou. Men typically don't go hunting without a woman to tend to the camp, so Atanarjuat reluctantly agrees to let Puja, Uqi's sister, come along in Atuat's place. During the hunt, Atanarjuat and Puja begin to enjoy each other's company, and eventually they make love. Atanarjuat now has two wives.

Later, back at the main camp, tensions grow between Atuat and Puja. Puja leaves all the work for Atuat to do and struts around like the queen of the camp. Then one night in the large tent they all share, Puja seduces Atanarjuat's older brother, Aamarjuaq, but the two of them are caught in the act. Puja is driven out of the camp and forced to return to Sauri and Uqi. The old tensions flare again quickly. Sauri belittles his son for allowing Atanarjuat to win Atuat in the punching contest, but Uqi is determined to strike the final blow. He and Sauri begin to discuss the possibility of murder. They devise a plan that will end with the deaths of Atanarjuat and Aamarjuaq.

The plan begins with Puja's return to Atanarjuat's camp. She looks as though she has been crying all night, and she sobs and begs for forgiveness. She asks to be allowed to return, and she promises to help with the camp chores more in the future. When Atanarjuat returns from hunting, however, he tries to drive her away; only the assurances from his first wife, Atuat, that all is forgiven keep him from striking Puja. But at last everyone agrees to put the past behind them and try to live as a family once again. The brothers, tired from their hunt, decide to get some sleep while the women and children go off to search for some eggs. Puja remains in the camp to start the cooking.

But behind some rocks, Uqi and his gang are waiting. They watch as Puja places a sock on the outside of the tent wall, marking the place where Atanarjuat lies inside. She places another sock to mark Aamarjuaq's position. Then she slips away.

Uqi and his gang sneak up and surround the tent. At Uqi's signal, the tent is collapsed on top of the sleeping brothers. Uqi rams his spear through the tent wall where the sock marks Atanarjuat's location; the sharp point just barely misses Atanarjuat inside. Uqi and the others stab again and again, trying to kill anything that moves in the tent. At last, Uqi sees a large shape moving beneath the skin and thrusts his spear through it. Aamarjuaq cries out, "Little brother! I'm stabbed! Get away!"

With his brother dying, Atanarjuat is clearly outnumbered and doomed. Just then an unearthly voice cries out: "Atanarjuat angajuata aqpakpasii! Atanarjuat's brother is running after you!" The attackers freeze, and Uqi suddenly sees his murdered grandfather, Kumaglak, standing beside him. Uqi hurls his spear at the ghost, which disappears. The distraction gives Atanarjuat an opportunity to escape, however, and he bursts from beneath the collapsed tent, totally naked. He dashes across the frozen sea ice, the attackers sprinting after him.

The women return from gathering eggs just in time to see Atanarjuat running naked across the ice. Uqi throws his spear at Atanarjuat but misses. The attackers maintain their pursuit, determined to kill Uqi's rival.

Atanarjuat runs as fast as he can, barely widening the gap between himself and his pursuers. His feet, slashed by the sharp ice, leave bloody prints in the snow. His attackers are fully dressed and fully armed. They chase Atanarjuat away from land, knowing that he will eventually succumb to the cold and collapse, giving them the chance to kill him at last.

After running steadily for some time, struggling to ignore the pain in his feet and the chill in his bones, Atanarjuat comes upon a large crack in the ice. It is wide and deadly; falling into the ocean would mean certain death. But the attackers are closing in on him. Just as Atanarjuat seems to have no options left, he sees a person standing on the other side of the lead. An illusion? A spirit? The person urges him to jump. Atanarjuat sprints toward the lead and hurls himself into the air. He soars over the black water and lands with a grunt on the other side. The person is gone, but his voice urges Atanarjuat to run to Sioraq, an island off in the distance. Atanarjuat resumes his steady stride and continues across the ice.

When Uqi arrives with his men at the lead, he is determined to prove that he is every bit the man that Atanarjuat is. He dashes toward the same spot where Atanarjuat leapt, but realizes at the last moment that he cannot make it. He tries to stop, but his momentum skids him across the ice. He dumps awkwardly into the water and screams for his companions to fish him out. Once back on solid ice, trembling with cold and fear and rage, he orders his friends to fetch the dogs. They will pursue Atanarjuat by sled.

Atanarjuat, still running, finally nears the island of Sioraq. An elder from Igloolik, Qulitalik, is camping there with his wife, Niri-uniq; they had left Igloolik years before, when Sauri took control of the camp. Now they are happy and content with their own company and the delightful manners of their twelve-year-old adopted daughter, Kigutikarjuk. They hunt ducks and gather eggs, enjoying the abundance of food they find around them.

Meanwhile, Uqi and his men have rounded up the dogs and have driven their sleds to the lead. They follow the crack to its end and return on the other side, looking for the bloody footprints that will mark Atanarjuat's path. But they find no footprints; they complain that the blood must have drained down through the snow. Still, they know no one can survive on the ocean ice without clothing, boots, and hunting tools. They agree that they are now looking for Atanarjuat's corpse.

On Sioraq, Qulitalik spots a moving shape on the ice. At first his wife declares that it is a bear, but then they realize that it is a man, naked and injured. They run toward him and arrive just as Atanarjuat collapses unconscious on the ice. They carry him back to their camp and cover him with warm caribou hides.

When Atanarjuat regains consciousness, he explains that people are trying to kill him. The young Kigutikarjuk climbs a nearby hill to watch for intruders, while her mother rubs seal fat on Atanarjuat's shredded feet. Atanarjuat tells them it is Sauri's son who is after him, and Qulitalik realizes the danger they are in. He hides Atanarjuat in a pile of seaweed on the beach and prepares to meet Uqi and his men.

When they arrive, they demand to know if Atanarjuat has come this way. Qulitalik and his family insist they have seen no one. Uqi glares at Qulitalik, trying to determine whether he is telling the truth. He sends his men to search the tent and check the sea ice for signs of blood. They find nothing.

Ultimately, the attackers conclude that no one could run this far without clothing and boots. Qulitalik, in an effort to appear nonchalant, offers Uqi and his men some food. The men eat and then move off to search for Atanarjuat's body.

When Uqi returns to Igloolik, frustrated that he could not find evidence of Atanarjuat's death, he plots to take Atuat as his wife — as had been promised years before. He has never gotten over losing her in the punching contest, and he plans to force her to marry him. But when he discusses his plan with his father, the camp leader refuses to allow it, pointing out that Atanarjuat might be alive. "We don't steal women in this camp," he says. Uqi is bitterly angry, apparently thwarted by his rival even in death.

Back on Sioraq, Atanarjuat heals slowly, gradually regaining his strength. But strange omens begin to happen: an egg he reaches for hatches at that instant, and a sharp rock mysteriously appears under the bed. Atanarjuat has strange and vivid nightmares, and

Qulitalik tells him that something is still chasing him. The attackers are long gone, but the evil spirit that impelled them continues to pursue Atanarjuat.

At the main camp, Uqi's determination to marry Atuat takes a dark turn. With his sidekicks along for muscle, he follows Atuat and waits until she is alone. Then they attack her and hold her down while Uqi rapes her.

On Sioraq, a roaring wind rises swiftly and knocks Qulitalik's tent flat. Atanarjuat jumps up, still half asleep, ready to fight whoever might be attacking. When he realizes that it was just another omen, he offers to leave the camp. He doesn't want the evil spirit to harm Qulitalik and his family, and he aches to return to his wife and son. But Qulitalik insists that Atanarjuat wait until the time is right and his feet are fully healed. Atanarjuat faces more powerful forces that he knows, and Qulitalik can see the danger ahead. They pack up their camp and cross the ice to Baffin Island.

Sauri has ordered that his camp be moved as well. Uqi continues to demand that Atuat be his wife, but Sauri still will not allow it. Father and son drive their separate dogsleds, Uqi whipping his dogs mercilessly in anger.

Back at Qulitalik's camp, Atanarjuat has come to realize the danger he faces from the evil spirit. But he also knows that he must make his stand — he must face the evil spirit before he faces his rivals at home — so he asks Qulitalik to help him. Qulitalik, convinced that Atanarjuat now knows what he is doing, gives him a small walrus-skin pouch. He tells Atanarjuat to put into it droppings from every animal. "Caribou, lemming, fox. . . . The more the better. It will help you when you need it." He also gives Atanarjuat a rabbit's foot.

At last Atanarjuat is ready to begin his journey. Qulitalik tells him to exercise his mind: "Here . . . hold this rock in your left hand all day. When you know what to do with it, you can put it down." He continues with his advice, bringing the power of helping spirits fully into the situation. "Remember . . . (peeps like a snow bunting) when your pouch goes like that it's time to come back. Give thanks to the four winds from the highest peak and shout, 'It's done!'"

Atanarjuat leaves Sioraq, and, as Qulitalik predicted, the evil spirit challenges him promptly. As Atanarjuat walks, he sees a dead polar bear carcass. When he approaches, however, it rises; it is a bear's head on a human body. The creature growls hideously and grabs Atanarjuat with clawed human hands. It knocks Atanarjuat to the ground, but then Atanarjuat remembers the rock in his hand. He hurls it at the creature and hits it in the face. The beast moans—and disappears.

Atanarjuat continues, his journey marked with nightmares, visions, and communications with the spirit world. In one nightmare, images of the naked Puja mingle with flashes of Aamarjuaq, his chest covered in blood. Aamarjuaq accuses Atanarjuat of running away instead of helping him fight off the attackers. Atanarjuat sobs, confused; as the older brother, Aamarjuaq would be expected to help Atanarjuat, not the other way around.

In a daytime vision, Qulitalik catches up with Atanarjuat and chats with him reassuringly. "Don't worry," Qulitalik says, "you finally did the right thing! (confident, positive smile) Now give me the rabbit's foot and your pouch and we can go home." But something about Qulitalik's manner is too eager, and Atanarjuat becomes suspicious. At the last instant, he pulls the amulets back, refusing to give them to Qulitalik. With a thunderclap, the false Qulitalik reverts to the man-bear and screams wildly. The wind howls as the beast raises a harpoon and slams it into Atanarjuat's chest. Atanarjuat falls to the ground. "Death come upon you!" the evil spirit screams. Atanarjuat's world goes black.

At the other camp, everyone is working to set up the tents and arrange the gear. Uqi approaches Atuat kindly and offers her some new skins for herself and her son. "It's getting colder now," he says, trying to provide for her. But he can't resist adding: "I only want to help since you don't have a man to look after your needs." Atuat recoils. "'No husband'? How dare you say that to me? You who killed him and his brother! (storms off muttering) I'll let you know when we need skins."

The magic continues. Atuat has strong feelings—even visions—

that Atanarjuat is alive and coming home. Atanarjuat, recovering from his contact with the evil spirit, hears his pouch peeping like a snow bunting, and he breaks into a wide smile. "It's . . . done!" he says. He returns to Qulitalik and his family, confident that he has now developed both the strength and the spiritual insight to overcome his foes.

Atanarjuat continues to live with Qulitalik and his family on Sioraq, helping them hunt for food. But he also spends his time fashioning caribou-antler crampons, which will allow his feet to keep their grip on slippery ice. He also carves a caribou-antler club, and he shows the crampons and club to Qulitalik. Qulitalik warns Atanarjuat that Uqi and his friends are strong — and that the evil spirit Tuurngarjuaq gets stronger with each encounter. "Well, Uqi is just a man like me," Atanarjuat says. "I can stand up to him. But Tuurngarjuaq? Last time I almost didn't live." Qulitalik stares intently at Atanarjuat. "Don't forget to give me the rabbit's foot the last thing before you go," he says.

The evil in Uqi's heart now takes hold for good. During a seal hunt, when Sauri is waiting alone at a breathing hole for his quarry to appear, Uqi approaches him. With a swift movement and no hesitation, Uqi stabs his father. "You've been in my way too long," Uqi says. "Atuat is mine now." Uqi takes his father's place as the leader of the camp.

It does not take long before Atuat's situation becomes serious. Her clothes are threadbare, she has little food, and her oil lamp is running dry. Not certain of Atanarjuat's fate, she decides to give herself to Uqi — it's the only way to save herself and her family. At that moment, back at Qulitalik's camp, a strange noise bubbles from the oil lamp. Qulitalik hears the voice of Panikpak, the widow of the original slain camp leader. She tells him that it is time for them to return. Qulitalik tells the others that they must go now to Igloolik. Atanarjuat gives the rabbit's foot to Qulitalik. "Here. . . . You can have this now," he says.

The next morning, Qulitalik sends a spirit rabbit to Igloolik. Later that day, Uqi sees a rabbit hopping right at his feet. He catches it and asks Atuat and Panikpak to join him for a rabbit-meat meal. They just walk away. Back in his igloo, Uqi eats the entire rabbit himself, sharing it with no one. Then Uqi falls into a deep sleep, spasms once, and then awakes. "That was the best nap I ever had!" he says. "Myumm! That rabbit was delicious!"

Later, Atuat begins to move in with Uqi. She and her son look dejected, but she is resigned to her fate. Then Atuat notices a dog team off in the distance. Uqi steps forward to greet the newcomer, and Puja cries out, "Atanarjuat kisimi manusinaarqpajuvuq! [Only Atanarjuat wears his parka with a white design in front!]" Atuat pushes to the front of the crowd. As the stranger comes closer, Atuat recognizes him: "Atanarjuat!!" she shouts. She runs forward, with her son close behind. She leaps into Atanarjuat's arms, and they both topple to the snow, laughing and crying. Their son piles on as well. The reunited family rejoices in their love.

Then Atanarjuat stands and looks at his wife. Her clothes are old and ugly. "When did I ever let you wear clothes as poor as these?" he asks. He cuts her amauti off her and presents her with a beautiful new one.

Back with the crowd, Puja has to decide which side to support this time. After seeing Atuat's new clothing, she makes her move. "Husband!" she cries. "I can't believe you are still alive!" She runs across the ice toward him. "I am not surprised you don't believe it," Atanarjuat replies. He slices open her amauti as well, leaving her topless — but then makes no move to replace it. He just leaves her standing there, her smile gradually fading to humiliation. "Go back to your friends," Atanarjuat says. "Now you are dressed as you deserve."

Some time later, when Atanarjuat has everything arranged, he sends Atuat and their son to wait with Qulitalik, who also has returned from Sioraq. Atanarjuat asks Atuat to send Uqi and his friends over, so they can eat together. "I want to eat first with Uqi, to remove this heaviness from our hearts." As she leaves, Atanarjuat pours some water over his igloo floor, creating a sheet of dangerously slick ice.

At last, Uqi arrives at Atanarjuat's igloo, with his friends a distance behind. Both Uqi and Atanarjuat greet each other cheerfully, seemingly determined to put their tensions behind them. Eventually, Uqi and his friends are seated on the slippery floor of Atanarjuat's igloo. They chat and eat voraciously, and then Atanarjuat excuses himself and steps outside.

Once outside the igloo, Atanarjuat ties on the antler crampons and hefts the antler club. Then he reenters the igloo and stands tall on the steady crampons. Uqi and his men try to stand, but they fall on the ice. Atanarjuat strikes one of the men on the shoulder with his club, and the other sidekick slips on the ice and hits his head on the floor. But Uqi is on his feet in an instant, knife drawn. He lunges at Atanarjuat, and both men fall to the floor. Uqi pins Atanarjuat to the floor and raises his knife, but Atanarjuat throws him off against the igloo wall. Now Atanarjuat jumps on top of Uqi and raises the heavy club.

Atanarjuat brings the club down with devastating force — just next to Uqi's head. Atanarjuat had a chance to kill his rival, but he chose instead to spare him. "The killing will stop," he says. "It ends here."

As the men emerge from the igloo, Qulitalik asserts his authority as an elder. "Whatever happened in there, only you four will know. But we are glad you're all alive. (To Atanarjuat) And that this killing will no longer carry on to others."

Qulitalik removes the walrus-tusk necklace from Uqi and gives it to Panikpak, the widow of the original camp leader. He orders everyone to gather that evening "to drive away the evil in our lives for so long."

That night, Qulitalik takes the pouch that Atanarjuat carried and uses his teeth to open it. As he does so, he begins to grunt like a walrus, steadily and with increasing volume. Amid the sound of barking dogs outside, the evil shaman Tuurngarjuaq enters the igloo. He seems relaxed and at home — until Qulitalik holds up the pouch. Then Tuurngarjuaq growls like a bear and lashes out at the people around him.

Qulitalik holds up the pouch and continues his grunting, like a bull walrus calling out a challenge. He circles Tuurngarjuaq, who growls deeply. An invisible blow from Tuurngarjuaq knocks Qulitalik backward, but when he gets up, Panikpak joins him, holding the walrus-tooth necklace and chanting. Panikpak and Qulitalik move slowly toward Tuurngarjuaq, chanting loudly. Then Qulitalik tosses some dust from the pouch over Tuurngarjuaq, who howls with agony. His bear's teeth fall out, bloody, and a powerful wind knocks him through the wall of the igloo. He is gone forever.

Everyone cheers, but Panikpak makes the next move. She insists that the evil brought into the camp by Tuurngarjuaq and passed along to Sauri, then Uqi and even Puja, be halted. "For the good of the people, and the healing we must do, it makes me sad to say that you, Uqi and Puja, my own grandchildren, and you, Pakak and Pittiulaq [Uqi's friends] whom I know since you are babies, must leave our camp and never return. . . . Now leave us. . . . I wish in my heart you can forgive yourselves as I forgive you, to find a better life somewhere else. Now go."

Uqi and the others stand and leave the igloo. Atanarjuat and Atuat's son rushes back in, scared by a snapping dog. The boy climbs into Panikpak's arms, and she starts to sing softly as the movie ends.

Inugpasugjuk's Version

The film version of the legend offers a fleshed-out and filled-in interpretation of the Atanarjuat story, with far greater detail and richness than the oral variants provide. One of the most pared-down versions was collected by the Danish explorer Knud Rasmussen when he visited the region in the early twentieth century (Rasmussen 1929, 298–99).[2] In the course of Rasmussen's several expeditions to the Arctic, he collected a wide range of materials from the Inuit, including tools, clothing, hunting implements, and stories. One of the legends he recorded involves the attack on Atanarjuat; it was told by an Inuit informant named Inugpasugjuk. This version is interesting for several reasons, beginning with the fact that the brothers' names are reversed; Atanârzuat is killed in the attack, and Aumarzuat escapes and is the central character of the story.[3]

The Fast Runner underscores the reason for the attack on the brothers' lives: the beautiful Atuat was promised in marriage to Uqi, but she falls in love with Atanarjuat. That love triangle heightens other tensions between Atanarjuat's and Uqi's family, a dangerous situation because the evil shaman at the start of the film tilts the power in favor of Uqi and his father.

In the version collected by Rasmussen, however, the cause of the deadly feud is not mentioned at all. The first sentence of the story leaps right into the assault: "Two brothers, Aumarzuat and Atanârzuat, lay sleeping one night in their tent, when they were attacked by enemies." The story does not say why these people were the brothers' enemies, nor does it specify how this feud began. This version also does not describe the attack in detail. It simply states that the brothers were attacked by enemies, with no elaboration or detail. In the second sentence, one brother is killed and Aumarzuat escapes.

It is also interesting that the film's most famous scene, in which Atanarjuat dashes naked across the ice to escape his attackers, does not take place in this version. Aumarzuat simply manages to escape and "make his way home to his parents' house." The focus of this version seems to be the attack and the retribution, not the means by which Aumarzuat manages to get away.

At his parents' house, Aumarzuat hides under some seaweed while his parents greet his pursuers. As also seen in the film version, the parents cook for the attackers in an effort to seem unconcerned, and eventually the attackers leave. "Aumarzuat then lay for some time to let his wounds heal, and when he was well again, he kept to places far from the dwellings of men, and hunted game for his parents." This sentence covers Aumarzuat's recovery in a brief moment, but *The Fast Runner* expanded this section to include the spiritual preparations and tests that paralleled the physical healing.

While he is healing, in the version collected by Rasmussen, Aumarzuat feels "a great desire to set out and take vengeance for the killing of his brother." His parents tried to talk him out of revenge — another point of departure for the film, in which Qulitalik and his wife work hard to prepare Atanarjuat for the battle he faces upon his return — and then he heads back to Igloolik. As the film shows as well, he is recognized by the particular markings on his parka, but the reunion in this version is hardly joyous. Immediately upon his return, Aumarzuat calls out his enemies: "I should like to fight while I am awake. Last time I was attacked while I slept. Let all my enemies come out if they dare." His enemies accept the challenge, and the fight begins. Aumarzuat kills two of his rivals immediately, and the others surrender. Aumarzuat takes the wives of the two men he killed, and he even kills another man for no apparent reason. The version offers something of an explanation that stands in stark contrast to the film: "He had, as it were, got into the way of killing; and thus he avenged the slaying of his brother."

Compared to the film version, the cast of characters in this version collected by Rasmussen is sparse. The storyteller, Inugpasugjuk, mentions the two brothers, the unnamed and unnumbered "enemies," the brothers' parents and specifically their mother, and the vanquished enemies' wives. No mention is made of other people who might have been involved in the feud, the attack, the healing efforts, or the final vengeance.

This version also makes no mention of spiritual forces. The miraculous escape, the healing, and the retribution are all accomplished through human means, without the intervention of shamans or supernatural entities of any kind. *The Fast Runner* clearly offers a departure from this version, showing how the conflict is carried out in both the human and the spiritual realms.

And perhaps the most significant aspect of Inugpasugjuk's version lies in the ending. After Aumarzuat rests and heals his wounds, he somehow develops "mighty strength." (It is unclear in this version whether he had that strength to begin with but was unable to use it because he was attacked while asleep, or whether he gained that strength during the healing he went through at his parents' house, "far from the dwellings of men.") He then returns to the village of his enemies and calls for a fight. He kills two men, and the others surrender out of fear. Then, as a final gesture of triumph, Aumarzuat claims the wives of the two men he had killed. On the trip back to his parents' house, he kills another man for no apparent reason. This ending, changed dramatically in the film version, offers a cautionary moral: "Behave badly, and look what will happen to you." The film version conveys a much more positive message.

Paniaq Version

Several other variants of the legend have been collected through the efforts of a project sponsored by the Igloolik Research Centre. One version was told by Igloolik elder Hervé Paniaq, who ultimately contributed to the writing of the *Fast Runner* script. The interview was conducted on March 24, 1990, by another elder, Louis Tapardjuk.

In Paniaq's version, Atanaarjuat lived at Pingiqqalik, an area not far from the current town of Igloolik. Again, no reason is given for the ongoing feud: "They had oppositions or enemies at the time." Paniaq's story mentions the clash between Atanaarjuat and his rivals over the dogsled, a scene shown in the film as well. In this scene, the enemies take Atanaarjuat's dog team and sled to intimidate and harass him. But Atanaarjuat runs after the sled and is able to overtake it. He forces the dogs to stop while his brother, "known for his strength," knocks the enemies off the sled and retakes it. In both this version and the film, this showdown over the sled serves to deepen the resentment between the two groups.

The feud simmers: "All through that time they did not get along [with the other hunters]." The brothers moved to Iksivautauyaak (Igloolik Point) for the spring hunting, each taking two wives with him. The story doesn't go into detail here, but the taking of two wives could also serve as an irritant in the small camp. The ratio of available women to available men was often tight and precarious, so a hunter taking two wives would not only be showing off, drawing attention to the fact that he could hunt so well he could feed three adults, but he also might threaten another man's ability to get a wife at all.

The attack scene receives little setup in Paniaq's version. The brothers go out hunting square-flipper seals, so their wives visit their own families. "This was the time it was decided that the two brothers must be killed." But this version offers a more thorough description of the attack scene than does the one collected by Rasmussen. Paniaq mentions that one of the wives placed stockings on the outside of the tents, to mark the places where the men slept inside. The attackers climbed onto the tents and stabbed through the material, killing Aamarjuaq. So the attack was made possible through the treachery of at least two of the wives. (It is unclear in this variant whether the betrayal was performed by only two or three of the brothers' wives. At one point, the story states that "the women would take their stockings outdoors and place them on the side of the tent," but when Atanaarjuat returns later he rewards one wife — "his second wife who was not involved in the set up" — with fresh clothes, while he gives the other only some raw skins. So the variant suggests that one of Atanaarjuat's wives was involved, and at least one of Aamarjuaq's wives.)

Guided by the stockings, the attackers kill Aamarjuaq, but unlike the version collected by Rasmussen, this one goes into greater detail about the escape. While the attackers were stabbing Aamarjuaq, an old woman yells "Atanaarjuap angayuata arpapasii" ("Atanaarjuat's older brother is running for you"). This variant also describes the iconic run across the ice in some detail. In this variant, Atanaarjuat is sleeping in his own tent, separate from his brother. The brother is killed, but Atanaarjuat is able to escape. He dashes across the ice, naked, toward the island of Siuqat (Sioraq). Paniaq goes on to describe the bloody footprints in the snow, Atanaarjuat's leap across the lead in the ice, and his rescue by the elderly couple and their granddaughter. It also notes Atanaarjuat's refuge in the seaweed and the way the couple greeted the attackers, fed them casually, and denied ever seeing Atanaarjuat. Eventually, the attackers depart.

Atanaarjuat stays on the island until summer, when he moves with the elderly couples and their grandchild to a place called Tasirjuaq, where they anticipate good caribou hunting. They catch an abundant supply of caribou, which provides them with clothing and foot.

When winter returns, Atanaarjuat builds the igloo in which he plans to trick his enemies, just as in the movie. He floods the area to make the footing slippery, and he has a pair of boots made with caribou antlers attached to provide traction. He also makes a caribou-antler club.

Then he returns to Igloolik by dogsled, taking with him a fresh set of clothing as a gift for the wife who was not involved in the attack plot. As he approaches, in a scene also portrayed in the film, the wife sees him coming and recognizes him by his parka. When they reach each other, he tears off her old, tattered clothing and replaces them with the new ones he has brought. When the other wife arrives, the one who had betrayed him, he tears her clothes off as well, but then hands her a pile of skins so she can make another set later.

Then he tells everyone about all the caribou he has cached back at his camp. He invites everyone to come over for a feast, even hinting that they will be able to take extra meat home with them. His enemies accept his offer and arrive at the camp. Just as in the film, once everyone has eaten his fill, Atanaarjuat takes out the club and begins to strike his enemies. The slippery footing prevents them from escaping, and Atanaarjuat clubs them all to death.

The cast of characters is somewhat larger in this variant than in the one recorded by Rasmussen. In addition to the two brothers, Paniaq mentions each brother's two wives, the enemies, the brothers' father and mother, and the people living on Siuqat. (This variant has two couples living on Siuqat with their grandchild, although later in the story this seems to shift. Paniaq mentions "the two couples" greeting the attackers, but later refers to "the elderly couple," "the wife," and "the man." The shift might be due to the use of English; the original references to "two couples" might actually refer to two people who formed a couple.)

The role of supernatural forces in this variant is mentioned only briefly, in two places. At one point, the story describes how the brothers' mother was forced to eat only walrus ribs, all the other food being claimed by the enemies. The story suggests that a steady diet of walrus ribs resulted in the strength that the brothers possessed: "so the strengths of his two sons were connected to the diet she ate." This might be a reference to nutrition, suggesting that eating a lot of meat will result in a healthy and strong baby. But the Inuit diet consisted of a great deal of meat and very little plant material, so it is not likely that this interpretation is on target. Inuit audiences would know, however, that the behavior of a mother during pregnancy would affect her children through a kind of contagious magic. By eating the rib meat of the walrus, the brothers' mother was imbuing her children with the qualities of a walrus, and those qualities include significant strength.

Another possible reference to the supernatural in this variant involves Atanaarjuat's escape from his would-be killers. Just as the attackers are about to stab through the fabric of Atanaarjuat's tent, an old woman calls out: "Atanaarjuap angayuata arpapasii" ("Atanaarjuat's older brother is running for you"). The story does not state who the old woman is, and she seems to appear out of nowhere. Her warning is also strange, in that the attackers have just killed Atanaarjuat's older brother. Either she is a crafty onlooker who thinks of something disturbing to say just to distract the attackers or she represents a spiritual force that intervenes to direct the action on the ground.

And the ending of this variant is more explicit than it was in Inugpasugjuk's version. In Paniaq's story, Atanaarjuat builds an igloo and ices the snow around it. (The order of events is unclear in this variant, but the actions are described in some detail.) He then feeds his enemies, straps on the caribou crampons he made (that step is implied), and kills his foes with his pre-made club. There is no discussion of Atanaarjuat taking his enemies' wives or killing anyone else; the story simply ends with the revenge killings.

Kupaaq's Version

Another variant of the Atanarjuat legend was told by Michel Kupaaq in an interview with Therese Ukaliannuk on March 6, 1990. This version begins with a description of Atanaarjjuat's rock near Igloolik Point and describes how the brothers would wait on their stone benches for their whale carcasses to drift ashore.

Kupaaq goes on to link the brothers' hunting prowess with the feud: "As the two brothers were successful hunters, the rest of the hunters felt jealous about their hunting ability." This jealously was perhaps bolstered by the brothers' use of floats and their deep understanding of ocean currents to cause the hunted whales to drift in to shore; ordinary hunters, on catching a bowhead or other whale, would have to paddle a kayak back to shore with the animal in tow. Many kayaks and a lot of hard work were often required to bring the whale to shore, but the brothers merely lounged on their stone seats and waited for the food to come to them. That their hunting practices served as a cause for the murder is suggested in the story: "The rest of the hunters knew that once the ice had left that the two brothers would again practise their mastery hunting skills to kill bowhead whales and wait for the floats to show up on the horizon while they waited on their stone benches." Kupaaq also notes that each brother took two wives.

The attack follows the same lines as the previous variants. The wives mark their husbands' sleeping places with stocking on the outside of the tent, and the attackers jump onto the tent and knock it down, stabbing through the skin where the stockings were. Once again, however, an old woman interferes, shouting "Atanaarjuap angajuata arpapaasi!" ("Atanaarjuat's older brother is running for you!"). Aamarjuaq is outnumbered and killed, but Atanaarjuat is able to escape, running onto the ice without any clothing on.

In this version, Atanaarjuat's footspeed saves him once again. He outruns his pursuers, but the ice slashes at his feet, leaving a bloody trail. Atanaarjuat leaps across the lead in the ice, thwarting his pursuers, who return to their camp.

As before, two elders on Siuraq see Atanaarjuat coming. This variant shows a bit more active cunning on the elders' part; to hide his trail, they cut out snow blocks containing the bloody footprints and turn them upside down, leaving nothing but white snow on the surface. Then they hide Atanaarjuat under the seaweed, a detail common to all the variants I found. Also common to all the variants is the action taken by the elders to convince the attackers that no one had joined them: they deny all knowledge and cook a meal as though they have nothing to hide. Once the attackers leave, the elders begin to nurse Atanaarjuat back to health.

Kupaaq's version, like Paniaq's, describes how the elders and Atanaarjuat moved to a caribou-hunting area to cache meat for the winter. In this version as well, Atanaarjuat builds an igloo and waters the grounds around it, making the area slippery. Atanaarjuat begins his preparations for his return to Igloolik, including packing some food and a set of clothing for the wife who did not betray him.

The reunion in Igloolik also echoes the two previous oral versions and the film. Atanaarjuat approaches Igloolik and is identified by the loyal wife, although the detail about Atanaarjuat's distinctive parka is omitted. Atanaarjuat gives the loyal wife the fresh clothing, tearing the old and worn-out clothes off her body. When the disloyal wife greets him, he tears her clothes off as well, but leaves her naked and humiliated. "He gave her skins that she would be able to make her clothing with and sent her on to her place — for he had no intentions of returning her as his wife."

The showdown progresses in the now familiar pattern. Atanaarjuat invites his rivals to his camp for a meal, with the added incentive in this version of caribou hides they can use for clothing. Kupaaq adds a detail explaining why both sides of the conflict, Atanaarjuat and his enemies, felt confident in meeting. Atanaarjuat considers himself safe as long as he is awake, and the enemies arrive together in one formidable group.

Kupaaq also mentions the caribou-antler crampons and the club. Atanaarjuat feeds his rivals until they can eat no more, then steps outside to put on the crampons. He returns and clubs his enemies.

Some run outside, but Atanaarjuat remains in the igloo in this version, checking the pulses of his prostrate foes. When he finds one still alive, he swings the club again. Then he goes outside and finds the others struggling on the slippery ice. He kills them as well.

In an ending similar to the story Rasmussen collected, but adding details missing from the Paniaq version, Kupaaq's variant has Atanaarjuat taking his rivals' wives as his own. He also "adopts" their children, although the language makes it sound more like slavery: "As for the sons that he had left fatherless, he had them working to serve him as well. Some he gave the task to harpoon, while others carried things for him, and some who only had to pick up things" (Kupaaq 1990).

The characters in this variant include the usual list — the brothers (but not their parents), the attackers, the wives, the elderly couple(s) and their grandchild at Siuraq, and the potentially supernatural old woman whose call distracts the killers enough for Atanaarjuat to get away.

Commonalities and Differences

In all the variants, the legend is highly situated, focusing specifically on the Igloolik region. Atanarjuat and his family live on Igloolik Island and camp at the point of land called Iksivautaujaak, which is a direct reference to the stone seats that Atanarjuat and his brother used. The brothers would paddle their kayaks out to sea, kill a bowhead whale at just the right place in the currents, and then return to Iksivautaujaak. There they would sit on their stone benches and wait for the currents to carry the enormous carcass to their shore, right at their feet.

When Atanarjuat and his brother are attacked, Atanarjuat runs across the ice toward Sioraq, a small island that lies off the Igloolik coast. The distance is both impressive and plausible; someone trying to escape murderers on Igloolik might see Sioraq off in the distance and attempt to make it that far. But most people who tried such a maneuver — especially while naked and barefoot — would not make it. The cold would sap their strength and blur their judgment, and the ice would slash their feet. But Atanarjuat was an extraordinary runner, and in some versions he received help from the spirit world; with that help and the fortunate proximity of Qulitalik and his family, he was just able to survive.

Interestingly, these three variants are remarkably similar in their core content; the scope of the details is the primary difference among them. As I have shown, however, the movie script differs from these variants in significant ways. As Cohn put it:

> We had put togther a five-man scriptwriting team — Apak, Zach, Qulitalik, Paniak and me — to turn Apak's treatment, based on eight elders' story versions, into a 115-page screenplay. These Inuit legends are like riddles or poems, with a few key details but not much character development. To make Atanarjuat into a believable movie, as if real people had lived through these events, Apak had to imagine characters, emotions and motivations that were not in the original legend. If a man ran naked for his life across the ice chased by people trying to kill him, who were these people and why would they be doing this? When Apak tried to imagine these events happening, he realized it must have been a love story, a triangle of jealousy and revenge, with some evil shamanic force behind it, so that's the story he wrote. (Igloolik Isuma Productions 2002, 25)

CHAPTER SIX

Reviews and Awards

When Zacharias Kunuk, Norman Cohn, and the other members of the Isuma team were working on the *Fast Runner* project — dealing with funding delays, changes in the cast, the need to focus on a hundred things at once — they were confident that they were creating something special. That confidence was rewarded once the film was released: Despite the use of the Inuktitut language, despite the use of amateur actors, despite the focus on a part of the world generally ignored by most societies, *The Fast Runner* received numerous major awards and acclaim from a broad array of critics. Some of the awards and comments were mentioned in this book's introduction, but I'll go into greater detail here.

Perhaps the most prestigious award earned by the film was the Camera d'Or award, given by the Cannes Film Festival. Awarded to *The Fast Runner* in 2001, the Camera d'Or (Golden Camera) award is given to the best first feature film presented in one of the Cannes selections — Official Selection, Director's Fortnight, or International Critic's Week. The recipient is chosen by an independent jury and the award is presented during the closing ceremonies of the festival. When asked to speak after receiving the award, Isuma producer Kunuk delivered his acceptance speech entirely in Inuktitut.

In addition to the Camera d'Or, *The Fast Runner* received a host of other honors in 2001. The film was awarded six Genies, the Canadian equivalent of the Oscars,, including one for Best Picture. The other categories topped by *The Fast Runner* were Best Director, Best Screenplay, Best Original Score, Best Editing, and the Claude Jutra Award, which is presented each year to the best picture by a first-time film director. Only two films in the half-century history of the Genies have won both the Claude Jutra and the Best Picture awards.

In addition to the Camera d'Or and half a dozen Genies, *The Fast Runner* earned awards at film festivals around the world. It was co-winner of the Guardian Award for Best New Director at the Edinburgh International Film Festival and was named Best Canadian Feature Film at the Toronto International Film Festival. At the Flanders International Film Festival in Ghent, *The Fast Runner* was awarded the "Grand Prix of the Flemish Community" for best film. The movie also received the Special Jury Prize and the Prix du Public at the Festival International du Nouveau Cinema et des Nouveaux Medias de Montreal. And it earned CTV's Best of Fest Award at Next Fest 2001, the Digital Motion Picture Festival.

The Fast Runner also was Canada's selection for the Foreign Language Oscar award. Each country may nominate only one per year, and 2001 marked the first year in which Canada nominated a film in a language other than French.

In 2002 the film earned even more awards. It received the Best Film award at the Imagine NATIVE Media Arts Festival, the Best Feature Film honors at the Santa Fe International Festival, and the Best Feature Film award at the San Diego International Film Festival. It also was given the Audience Award at the Newport International Film Festival, the Audience Award at the Lake Placid Film Forum and the Best Film, Best Actor, and Best Actress honors at the American Indian Film Festival, and was named Best Feature-Length Mountain Fiction Film at the Banff Mountain Film Festival.

In addition to its long list of awards, *The Fast Runner* received praise from a wide range of sources. Jerry White, an associate professor of English and Film Studies at the University of Alberta, published an exceptionally well-timed interview with Kunuk in the December 2001 issue of *CinémaScope*. A doctoral fellow in comparative literature at the time, White prefaced the interview with an informative, if someone error-prone, description of the role *The Fast Runner* played in the Canadian cinematic landscape. His strongest contribution in this introduction explored the challenge *The Fast Runner* presented to established notions of what constituted Canadian films, indigenous films, and video projects.

This challenge was manifested in the funding difficulties the film's producers encountered by trying to create a full-length, full-budget film about indigenous culture in a language other than English or French. White notes that the new thinking required by *The Fast Runner* is similar to the problem presented by Quebecois cinema, and "*Atanarjuat's* international circulation will further complicate a discussion of the national cinemas north of the 49th parallel." (The interview White conducted with Kunuk, while well-intentioned, attempts to beg specific answers from Kunuk in a way that the producer adamantly resists. White asked, for example, "Do you think your relative isolation has anything to do with why there's such a vibrant culture in Igloolik?" to which Kunuk answered, "No" (White 2001, 33). The interview does a good job, however, of eliciting brief glimpses into the funding crisis that *The Fast Runner* encountered during production.)

In general, most of the commentary about *The Fast Runner* focused on a specific set of themes that can be helpful in understanding the film more fully.

Showing a Culture

Some reviews of the film focused on its approach to educating audiences about Inuit culture and life in the Arctic. Rather than introduce audiences to central facets of Inuit culture one at a time, making sure each piece is solid before moving on, Kunuk and Cohn allow viewers to learn by observing the real-time unfolding of activities, habits, rhythms, and patterns around them. The approach can be bewildering at times, but the blending of narrative and cultural content affords viewers an immediate and visceral experience that transcends linear understanding. Writing in the *London Daily Telegraph*, S. F. Said accurately depicted the film's storytelling power:

> While the film gives rich insights into a fascinating culture, it is of far more than anthropological interest. It is totally compelling, dramatic, accessible; it is as if you have known this story all your life. *Atanarjuat* seems to tap into a vein of narrative, a universal

style of storytelling that deals with human fundamentals: love and hate, jealousy and pride, fear and exultation. The results feel refreshingly pure and simple, especially compared with the superficiality of much Hollywood product. (Said 2001)

This approach requires some work on the viewers' part—the beginning of the film is often described as confusing, primarily because the story has not been neatly anchored and the characters are not directly introduced—but it allows the audience to learn in a very Inuit way. In *Eye Weekly*, critic Jason Anderson praises the film's approach to educating its audience, striking close to the reality that Kunuk and the other producers were working to convey. Noting Isuma's goal of appealing to a broad audience, Anderson observes that the producers "had to give viewers a new 'mental and visual vocabulary'" to enable them to understand the facets of Inuit culture presented in the film. He goes on to quote from an interview with Cohn, who points out that the film has to teach people how to watch while simultaneously presenting the story line and context to them. Resisting didactic approaches to that education, Kunuk and Cohn chose to adopt methods that are better suited to Inuit culture and to experimental video art. As Cohn puts it, "Inuit parents teach their kids by example and modeling," and then the film employs the same technique. The effect, says Anderson, is "the most significant achievement in recent Canadian cinema" that "lends even more terror and panic to that stark, lonely image of a naked man running for his life on frostbitten feet" (Anderson 2002).

Cohn's points about a nondidactic way of teaching refer to the typical way that Inuit parents educate their children and each other. Traditionally, they rely on showing much more than telling to get their lessons across. For example, during my research with Isuma, I observed an Inuit family taking part in a whale hunt. The teenage son was in the bow, harpoon at the ready. When the father steered the small boat close to a whale, the son hurled the harpoon—and missed. In many cultures, that error would be followed by a discussion of what the son did wrong, complete with explanations of how to do it right next time. But in this case, there was no discussion, no disappointment, no recriminations, no explanations. The father just circled the boat around and found another whale, another try. The son's job was to keep on trying, learning from his own mistakes and by watching the hunters around him until he got it right.

The acclamation surrounding Kunuk's portrayal of Inuit culture in the form of Inuit art triggered an explosion of articles in *Inuit Art Quarterly*, the premier publication devoted to Inuit art. The journal heralded every award and honor received by Isuma and Kunuk, including the National Aboriginal Achievement Award (noted in the Fall 2001 issue), the Banff Centre's National Arts Award (Winter 2002 issue), a litany of awards, as noted in the Spring 2002 issue, and Kunuk's appointment as an officer of the Order of Canada (Fall 2003 issue). The journal listed important airings of *The Fast Runner*, including showings at Documenta in Kassel, Germany, and screenings at the Toronto Film Festival, and noted the decision by Odeon to distribute *The Fast Runner* to theaters across Canada.

Inuit Art Quarterly also has published feature-length articles about Isuma and its work. One article, published in the spring of 1996 and foreshadowing only briefly the possible production of a full-length movie by Isuma, focuses on the ability of Inuit videographers to incorporate this new and non-Inuit medium into natural expressions of their culture. Written by Kathleen Fleming, a productive and insightful writer-researcher who works as a translator in Montreal, the article observes that video is "the latest example of how people can assimilate a medium effectively and use it for their own ends." Positioning itself squarely in opposition to those who would argue that video is non-Native and hence a destructive force in Native culture, the article goes on to point out that "the 'video movement' in Igloolik is not an anachronistic phenomenon arising inexplicably out of nowhere; it is the reasoned, organic response of a culturally strong community within a larger regional history of contact through telecommunications" (Fleming 1996, 27–28).

Sonia Gunderson, who has traveled extensively in the Arctic and is studying ways to present Inuit culture to others, wrote a feature piece for *Inuit Art Quarterly* that captured Kunuk's vision in a way many readers would understand. "Kunuk is a filmmaker with a compelling mission: to stem the tide of cultural erosion, by documenting the wisdom of the final generation of elders who lived on the land according to ancient custom, and to marry those traditions with the realities of modern Inuit life," she wrote (Gunderson 2004, 48).

Not long after *The Fast Runner* was released, the *Inuit Art Quarterly* published a feature-length article relaying the reactions to the film by the directors of the Inuit Art Foundation, which publishes IAQ. Several of the directors' comments focused on how the film crosses cultural boundaries on an educational mission. John Terriak of Nain, Labrador, for example, declared that the film "will help white people understand us more." Okpik Pitseolak of Iqaluit echoed that sentiment: "When I saw it for the first time, I thought that people would now understand the ways of the Inuit, how they lived, how they dressed, how they managed their dogs. I think that people with misconceptions about Inuit will now learn how it was. Even our youth will learn how their ancestors used to live. I am really happy about that." The reactions were not universally positive, however. Paulusie Kanayuk of Puvirnituq, Nunavik (Arctic Quebec), said the film "depicts Inuit ways — almost." He went on to say that he has never seen Inuit ways quite like those shown in the movie. And Mattiusi Iyaituk of Ivujivik, Nunavik, said he was concerned about what audiences would think after seeing the film: "I worry that, if the people who don't know anything about Inuit base their knowledge on this movie, the Inuit people might be considered cruel. For instance, there was a guy who was kicking and beating his dog, and at another point, a dog was caught up in the harness; it kind of hurt me to see it."

Immersion

Just as audiences are expected to learn by observing and figuring things out, they also are expected to absorb underlying meanings and significances just as though they were visitors to the Arctic.

The filmmakers do not spend time building connections, creating analogues, or building bridges that might help viewers understand the Arctic in terms of their own cultures. One point of the film is that audiences should understand the Arctic on Inuit terms. As A. O. Scott noted in the *New York Times*, "The first half-hour, which turns out to be a prologue to the main narrative, is a little confusing, in part because it immediately plunges into arcane Inuit lore. 'I can only say this story to someone who understands it,' a voiceover says at the beginning, and what follows slowly creates the conditions for that understanding" (Scott 2002).

Kenneth Turan, a critic for the *Los Angeles Times*, praises the film's ability to immerse viewers into both Inuit culture and the geographic landscape of the Arctic. Calling the film "the cinematic equivalent of adventure travel," Turan acknowledges that viewing it is challenging. "But the rewards for those who risk the journey," he notes, "are simply extraordinary." He describes how the film "deposits you deep within the compelling, unfamiliar culture of the native people of the Arctic North. And it tells a story of elemental passions, a mythic tale of courage and mendacity, of undying love and corrosive lust that can't help but hold our interest." Pointing out that the beginning of the film generates the same sense of confusion that a traveler would feel if dropping into that situation without preparation, he urges viewers to work through the confusion patiently. "Kunuk's unhurried pacing, his decision to duplicate the temporal rhythms of Inuit culture, make a willingness to give yourself over to the experience on its own terms essential." Soon, he insists, everything comes into sharp focus, brining the audience into the world presented in the film: "At the film's beginning, one of the tellers of this tale says, 'I can only sing this song to someone who understands it.' What's special about 'The Fast Runner' is that by its epic close, the select group includes us" (Turan 2002).

Complexity

Inuit culture is multifaceted, complicated, and confusing for many outsiders. In traditional Inuit life, scores of taboos regulated behavior in complex and difficult ways, and elders offered the guidance necessary to ensure happy deities, plentiful food, and protection from evil and the threat of harsh weather. Inuit made their way through life and established their identities, carved out their areas of expertise, and defended their place on the pecking order in concert with myriad challenges and expectations. Life in the Arctic was not merely a struggle for food and shelter; it included interacting with numerous forces, both earthly and supernatural, relationships that included what southerners might call casual sex or wife swapping, and age- and gender-based systems of organizing social interaction.

As A. O. Scott observed in his *New York Times* review,

Shot over six months and taking place across a span of many years, "The Fast Runner" captures the movement of the seasons above the Arctic Circle and the ways climate and the migratory patterns of animals influenced the traditional Inuit way of life. . . . You are so completely caught up in the codes and rituals of a nomadic, tribal society governed by complex ideas of honor and loyalty that it is easy to overlook the artistry that has put them before you. (Scott 2002)

Tom Dawson, a critic for the British Broadcasting Corporation, noted that the film's multiple strata succeed in encompassing cultural, historical, and social aspects of Inuit life:

Robustly acted by its Inuit cast, "Atanarjuat — the Fast Runner" succeeds as a mythic drama of good versus evil, in which the desires of an individual have to take secondary importance to the harmony of the group.

Yet it's also an impressively vivid and detailed depiction of a particular way of life: shelter is provided by carefully-constructed igloos, clothes are fashioned from animal skins, transport consists of husky-drawn sleds, whilst the staple food is walrus or seal meat.

And director Zacharias Kunuk also includes ritualistic events, such as a grieving ceremony and a bizarre head-thumping contest between two adversaries, which immerse us yet further into Inuit culture.

Cinematographer Norman Cohn shot this near three-hour odyssey on digital video before blowing it up to 35mm and, aided by the remarkable Arctic light, captures the forbidding expansiveness of the tundra landscapes, which dwarf the protagonists. There are some confusing time shifts in the initial scenes, yet "Atanarjuat" soon settles into its own rhythm, whilst the chase sequence involving a naked Atanarjuat being pursued on foot across the ice floes is genuinely extraordinary. (Dawson 2002)

Beauty

Many critics expressed admiration for the way the film depicts the beauty of the Arctic, an extraordinary accomplishment for a region many people consider desolate, bleak, and grim. A. O. Scott in his *New York Times* review noted that "Mr. Cohn, using a widescreen digital video camera, has discovered at least a dozen distinct shades of white, from the bluish glow of the winter ice to the warm creaminess of coats made of polar bear fur . . . . 'The Fast Runner' includes some unforgettable sequences, shot in the smoky interiors of igloos, out on the ice and in fields of yellow grass and purple clover during the brief spring thaw" (Scott 2002) This description of the film's visuals explodes the fallacy that the Arctic is a colorless wasteland of ice and rock. During my nine months in Igloolik, I was often captivated by the colorful beauty of the Arctic landscape, the rich warmth of a caribou-hide parka, the infinite shades of blue emanating from swooping and twisted icebergs on the shore. Scott recognized Isuma's ability to deliver the spectrum of sensual delight that Inuit have enjoyed for centuries.

Similarly, Nigel Andrews wrote in the *Financial Times* of London that at the Cannes Film Festival,

the dazzler from nowhere was *Atanarjuat the Fast Runner*. The locations are unsparingly harsh and beautiful. The camera work is stunning. The performances, all by Inuits, have a simple power that strikes us straight between the eyes, as fast and true as an arrow. . . . *Atanarjuat* speaks to today and of today. It depicts and celebrates a past that has bequeathed unchanged gifts to the present. . . . At the same time, it holds up a defiant paradigm to unthinking or insensitive progress. Telling stories of bygone times expresses the love of what made us, shaped us and can still teach us. (Andrews 2001)

And in *Variety*, critic Lisa Nesselson noted the techniques Isuma used to make the scenes vivid and beautiful, acknowledging the skilled videography in the harsh and screeching terminology that many pop-culture enthusiasts find enchanting:

Thousand year old tale of festering evil on the frozen tundra should find a warm welcome worldwide, particularly on the fest circuit. . . . [P]ic positively drips with an ineffable aura of genuineness. New York raised d.p., Norman Cohn, who has lived in Igloolik since 1985, positions the camera at dog and sled-runner level or arranges for it to glide across the snow during escape-and-chase scenes to excellent you-are-there effect. Thesps, many of them acting for the first time and dedicated to the idea of capturing their own history on film, inhabit their roles with oomph. (Nesselson 2001)

Even beyond an appreciation of the superficial beauty of the Arctic landscape, some critics noted the deeper, more personal beauty that the film captures and delivers. For example, Katrina Onstad describes the intimate beauty of the film in the conservative Canadian newspaper *The National Post*: "The film's surge of images creates another planet to unfamiliar eyes: yellow light bouncing off the inside of an igloo, dog teams leading hunters to frozen seals on tundra, women in facial tattoos under heavy animal skins that are somehow sexy, just a tug away from nakedness (despite the ice, *Atanarjuat* is one of the most erotic Canadian films ever)" (Onstad 2001).

Pacing

Not every critic gave the film high praise. In a review of the French film *Amélie* (whose full title is *Le fabuleux destin d'Amélie Poulain*) published in *Cinéma Scope* (December 2001), the Argentinean film critic Quintin places *The Fast Runner* in a category of films that "convey a sense of exoticism and bring a touch of local atmosphere and language providing, like ethnic food, that their tastes aren't too weird for the universal consumer" (Quintin 2001). The category is fair, and most filmgoers could probably name films that fall comfortably within it. But *The Fast Runner* is too immersed in Inuit culture, too deeply involved in both the quotidian and the extraordinary facets of Inuit life, to be dismissed as mainstream fare with slightly unusual seasonings. That the film has achieved worldwide acclaim while showing people eating raw seal meat carved straight from the slit-open carcass, otherworldly contests pitting ethereal polar bear spirits against ethereal walrus spirits in battles for the control of humans, and Atanarjuat filling a pouch with a wide assortment of animal droppings because of the potent powers they possess suggests more than just Hollywood dishes served with extra curry. *The Fast Runner* is a new kind of cinema, as many critics have suggested, and so it doesn't fit into pre-existing categories nearly that simply.

Another critic, Mark Dujsik, dismissed the film in a capsule review published on his website. He maintains that it will be remembered as the first Inuit movie, but that otherwise it is too dull to make a great cinematic impact. He acknowledges that the film is "expertly shot" by Norman Cohn and that its "images of vast, sweeping, snow-covered flatland are beautiful."

> On other levels, though, the movie drags. . . . [T]he screenplay so severely diminishes the fantastic and human elements of the story that it sometimes borders on unintelligible nonsense. . . . It moves at a snail's pace, which is fine near the beginning as we begin to learn about the culture, but that tempo continues even as events become more dire and urgent. . . . At three hours and with very little story or character development, there is plenty

of room for editing, and a much shorter cut surely would have resulted in a smoother, more focused narrative without sacrificing any of the cultural intrigue. There's a nice moral at the end, but it seems forced upon its characters. They probably don't even notice. (Dujsik 2002)

Dujsik's critique seems to suggest that he wants *The Fast Runner* to adhere to Hollywood's standards of fast scenes and exploding crescendos. As other critics — and the producers — have noted, however, the movie aligns itself not with Hollywood expectations but with the rhythms and style of Inuit culture. When a communicator attempts to reach across cultural borderlands, he finds himself beset with a galaxy of decisions. If he favors the culture he is describing at the expense of clarity and impact for his intended audience, then he risks the kind of criticisms that Dujsik offers. But if he favors the expectations and tropes familiar to the intended audience at the expense of accuracy, authenticity, and respect for the culture being depicted, then he risks producing a piece of popular entertainment with little insight or understanding, as *Enuk* did with the use of Styrofoam block igloos and Hawaiian actors representing Inuit characters.

Katherine Monk, writing in the *Vancouver Sun*, understood the intent behind the pacing more fully:

As the one of the first narrative features to emerge from the Canadian First Nations film tradition, Zacharias Kunuk's *Fast Runner* is nothing less than a complete revelation and reinvention of cinematic form. Stretched out over three hours, Kunuk slows his narrative pace to match the landscape and the aboriginal oral tradition. As a result, the story has a chance to sink in and stew — creating tension beneath the surface of these frozen frames. The beauty of the movie goes well beyond the incredible landscape, however, as it tells the story of Atanarjuat — a kid destined to take on the son of his father's rival. Set in an ageless time, before the white man sullied the North with European vice, the movie successfully translates myth to film without sacrificing anything in the process. A long voyage with a mighty big payoff, *Atanarjuat* is a definite "must-see." (Monk 2001)

The Fast Runner reflects the pace of life in the Arctic, which is slow more often than it is fast. (This theme permeates Kunuk's work. After observing the taping of an earlier video called *Saputi* (*Fish Weirs*), Sally Berger wrote: "In *Saputi*, as well as in other [Isuma] videotapes, living in harmony with family and friends means learning from, and responding to, the environment. Decisions such as when and where to build the saputi are based on temperature, rain, wind, tides, light, and animal migrating patterns" [Berger 1995, 108]) Nature and circumstances play a powerful role in determining what people can do and when they can do it. If a hunter is ready to go out but a storm is rising, then the hunter has no choice but to wait. If a family is hungry but the seals aren't showing up at their breathing holes, then the family must wait until other hunting opportunities arise. If someone wants to visit relatives in a distant town but the snowmobile isn't working, then the trip will be postponed until the machine can be repaired. After I was invited to join a family on the whale-hunting expedition, I had to wait for several days, duffel packed and survival suit ready, beyond the planned start of the trip. When I asked my host family about our departure, I was told that we would leave when the father of the family decided that the weather, tide, and other factors were satisfactory. He in turn received advice and guidance from more senior elders, who took responsibility for orchestrating the entire town's whale-hunting effort. My job was to wait quietly until the signal was sent for us to go. Circumstances force people in the North to learn patience; frustration is wasted effort. As Qulitalik says in *The Fast Runner*, "dreaming of ice won't make it freeze."

Praise

Several years before the *Fast Runner* project, Sally Berger observed the taping of *Saputi*, an earlier Isuma production. She noted in a 1995 article in *Felix* that "Sak Kunuk's video works have added a new dimension to the meaning of history and culture and mark the development of an important new form in moving images that is neither documentary, docu-drama nor fiction, but a combination of lived and recreated experience" (Berger 1995, 111). That vision has not lessened as time has passed, and for the most part, reviewers' responses to *The Fast Runner* were equally vigorous in their praise. Desson Howe, writing in the *Washington Post*, said the film is "as close to authentic myth as cinema has ever gotten" (Howe 2002). Margaret Atwood, a critic for the *Globe and Mail*, called Kunuk "Homer with a video camera" (Atwood 2002). Scott, the *New York Times* reviewer, added this about the film:

> *The Fast Runner* . . . is not merely an interesting document from a far-off place; it is a masterpiece. . . . It is, by any standard, an extraordinary film, a work of narrative sweep and visual beauty that honors the history of the art form even as it extends its perspective. . . . The most astonishing scene — during which Oki and his minions, after a brutal assault on their enemy's tent, pursue the naked Atanarjuat across a vast expanse of ice — has already become something of a classic, a word that will quickly be bestowed on the film as a whole. (Scott 2002)

Jim Hoberman, in the *Village Voice*, wrote: "Mysterious, bawdy, emotionally intense, and replete with virtuoso throat singing, this three-hour movie is engrossing from first image to last, so devoid of stereotype and cosmic in its vision it could suggest the rebirth of cinema" (Hoberman 2002). In the *Globe and Mail*, Rick Groen argued that "there are really only three things you need to know about *Atanarjuat*: (1) It is a superb film; (2) It is both intriguingly exotic and uniquely Canadian; (3) Although based on an ancient Inuit myth, and set on a frozen shore a thousand years ago, it speaks eloquent volumes about the way we live now" (Groen 2002).

The famous movie critic Roger Ebert also had high praise for the film: "*Atanarjuat (The Fast Runner)* is an astonishing epic film made by and about the Inuit peoples of the Canadian arctic, telling a story of a crime that ruptures the trust within a closely knit group, and how justice is achieved and healing begins. . . . [T]he three hour film was entirely shot on location, and shows the tenacity and creativity of a people making a home of a frigid wilderness" (Ebert 2002).

And the praise goes on: "A mystical arctic gem," Steven Rea, *Philadelphia Inquirer* (2002). "*Atanarjuat* emerges as a genuine delight," Andrew Pulver, *The Guardian* (2001). "Zacharias Kunuk's three-hour *Atanarjuat The Fast Runner* is an epic of a different order, and a landmark in its own right," Amy Taubin, *The Village Voice* (2001)."The movie's ritual world is astonishing," Brian D. Johnson, *Maclean's*. "A milestone . . . a fascinating cultural document," Liam Lacey, the *Globe and Mail* (2002).

But perhaps the highest station to express admiration for the film was the president of France. Jacques Chirac, on seeing *The Fast Runner*, had this to say: "J'ai suivi de très près l'extraordinaire aventure de ce premier film inuit qui a été primé à Cannes l'année dernière: *Atanarjuat, la légende de l'homme rapide*. La civilization inuit est une civilization passionante et ce film magnifique permet d'en entrevoir certains aspects" (www.atanarjuat.com). In rough translation, "I have followed very closely the extraordinary adventure of the first Inuit film, which received accolades at Cannes last year: *Atanarjuat, The Fast Runner*. The Inuit civilization is exciting, and this beautiful film allows us a glimpse into aspects of it."

CHAPTER SEVEN

Lifeways as Context

As a form of cultural expression, a film carries with it numerous simultaneous layers of meaning. On the surface, such elements as plot and character convey intended and unintended significance, focusing largely on specific points about individuals, their relationships, and the ways in which they deal with their circumstances. The action takes place within two sets of contexts, both of which illuminate, inform, and enrich the meanings available to the audience.

One set of contexts resides in the narrated event, to use the term Richard Bauman advanced (Bauman 1986, 2). The narrated event is the story that unfolds, the chronological actions of the characters within the setting of the tale. In *The Fast Runner*, the narrated event is the story of Atanarjuat and his struggles in Igloolik, the attack on him and his escape to Sioraq, and his efforts to return and end the longstanding feud. That story embraces a broad and intricate context about life in the Arctic five hundred years ago, which offers a great deal that is of significance to the audience.

The other set of contexts involves the narrative event, which Bauman contrasts to the narrated event. The narrative event is the context within which a story is told, the setting of the storytelling itself. For the Atanarjuat legend, the narrative event encompasses any situation within which the story is told to others: the warm darkness of an igloo, the bright gloss of the school gym, the comfortable environment of the family dinner table.

In the realm of filmmaking, the narrative event becomes somewhat more complicated than in oral storytelling. The telling of the story in film takes place in several distinct settings: the table at which the screenplay was written, the set on which the actors delivered their lines, the studio in which the raw footage was edited into a coherent format, the theater in which the film is played for an audience, and so on. Unlike in oral storytelling, these settings are disparate in time and space.

Both sets of contexts — in the case of *The Fast Runner*, the Igloolik of five hundred years ago and the Igloolik of today, among others — give shape and potency to the meanings of the film. In some cases those contexts are worlds apart, separated and colored by the extraordinary changes that have taken place in the Arctic during the past half-century. In other cases the sets of contexts resonate more closely, their similarities serving as a testament to the durability and relevance of Inuit culture.

Inuit audiences watching *The Fast Runner* often bring to the experience at least a partial lived understanding of the narrative event and a learned understanding of the narrated event to a greater extent than do audiences whose familiarity with the Arctic is more limited. An understanding of some of the more prominent if less familiar cultural elements in the film — including the games the characters play, the rituals of marriage, and the ways conflicts were mediated and resolved — might help non-Inuit audiences benefit from the contextual significance more fully.

Games

A pivotal scene in *The Fast Runner* involves the head-punching game between Atanarjuat and Uqi, for the unspoken prize of Atuat's hand in marriage. Such games were common in Atanarjuat's time and are still enjoyed today.

The games served an important social function. Life in a small Inuit camp could be trying and difficult. Everyone lived in close proximity to one other, often stuffed into warm igloos where physical contact was unavoidable and all conversations could be overheard. Offhand remarks and unintentional bumps and body language could lead to the flaring of tempers and the fostering of feuds.

Most of these clashes were superficial, and allowing them to fester into deep-seated resentment and even hatred could be devastating to the harmony of the small group. Because harmony was essential to everyone's survival and comfort, approaches were developed to defuse standoffs and settle quarrels without bloodshed or the fracturing of the camp. Many of these approaches are still in use today; I witnessed them during festivals and other events in Igloolik and other Inuit communities.

One of these approaches involved physical contests. Such contests were often used for fun and entertainment, but they could also be used to settle disputes. Just beneath the surface, however, lay the fact that it is difficult to perform some of these rituals without laughing — a powerful way to banish hard feelings and shrug off old grudges.

For men, the contests typically involved endurance, the ability to tolerate pain, or both. The contest shown in *The Fast Runner* was common: two men would face each other and take turns punching until one either collapsed or gave up. The classic (and much less dangerous) approach involved punching shoulders. Each man would punch his opponent on the upper-arm muscle with the fleshy part of his fist. The blows, gentle at first, would build in intensity until someone conceded. The contest between Atanarjuat and Uqi involves blows to the temple, a shorter and much more hazardous engagement. The intensity of this contest indicates both the seriousness of the stakes — they are fighting for the right to marry Atuat — and the degree to which the camp has shifted out of balance. Instead of a match designed to end with grins and sore shoulders, this one could lead to death.

A similar contest is called the "lip pull." For this, the rivals stood side-by-side, facing in the same direction. Each reached his inside arm behind his opponent's head and hooked a finger into the side of his mouth. At the signal, both men pulled back as hard as they could. This contest was painful; in part, it was a measure of how much a participant was willing to endure for the prize at stake, if any. The lip pull never lasted long. Both men would turn their heads and lean backward to ease the pressure on their mouths, so generally they both fell over backward in each other's arms, laughing, ending the game in a tie. It would be difficult to hold a grudge after that.

Other contests involved hanging from a horizontal pole by your knees and donning your parka while upside-down, kicking up from a "crab walk" position to hit a dangling object with your foot, crossing a certain distance touching the floor only with your toes and knuckles, and so on.

One of the classic contests for women involved throat singing; Atuat and Puja perform some throat singing in the film. Throat singing requires two voices, and the interactions between them form melodic tunes in harmonic ranges, higher than either person is singing. The singing actually sounds like rhythmic grunts and chants, carefully timed between the partners to generate the harmonic tones. Throat singing is often done for fun or to demonstrate prowess, but at times it is used as a contest of endurance among women. The grunting and chanting require a great degree of breath control, and many performers have to stop after just a few minutes. It also requires emotional control. The performers have to stand face-to-face, with their mouths close to each other, to create the harmonic sounds. Standing that close and looking someone straight in the eye while making guttural animal sounds is hard to do without laughing, and many throat-singing performances end with the women leaning on each other and laughing hysterically.

A verbal form of competition is also seen in the movie. When tensions rose high in an Inuit community, a special kind of drum-dance song was sometimes used to ease the mood. The goal of these songs, called *iviusiit*, was not to soothe but rather to explode the tensions with hyperbole and ridicule. The participants would make up verses insulting and humiliating their opponents, typically with the kind of exaggerated slander that can be seen in such contests as the "dozens" found in some African-American communities. The goal is to paint your opponent in a ridiculously bad light — call him a pathetic hunter, suggest that he can't satisfy his wife sexually, describe him as henpecked and cuckolded — and the job of the target of this abuse is to maintain an aloof and mildly bored air. Then the tables are turned, and the target becomes the insulting singer. These contests are designed to make petty squabbles seem insignificant — and to demonstrate that a thick skin is a good quality in a small and interconnected group.

In *The Fast Runner*, Atanarjuat's family and Uqi's family take part in this kind of contest. Along with the head-punching contest, however, these techniques for easing tensions and healing social wounds fail to overcome the vast rift that is developing in the camp. Perhaps because of the simmering evil presence of Tuurngarjuaq, perhaps because the time-honored systems of camp life are being ignored and overturned, and perhaps because Uqi is not the kind of guy who takes losing gracefully, these approaches only serve to push the overarching conflict into the background, where it can fester and grow more dangerous.

Other kinds of games were plentiful in the Arctic. Especially before the arrival of television, which came to Igloolik in 1981 after the community declined it twice out of concerns that southern programming would weaken Inuit culture, children had to occupy themselves indoors and out. One popular game resembled American baseball: children tried to hit a thrown ball with a stick and then run around some bases. Children also played hide-and-seek and a host of other games and pastimes to keep themselves busy and have fun.

One game shown in the movie is a form of tag, in which the person who is "It" must tag someone else. The twist is that the tag consists of touching that person with your bare hand on the bare skin underneath his or her parka. That maneuver generally requires the "It" whose turn it is to tackle someone in the snow and then slip a hand inside his or her coat. The game is popular with teenagers.

The person who is It is the wolf, and so tagging someone under their parka is called "wolfing." When the wolf touches bare skin under the parka, he or she declares "I 'wolf' you," meaning that the tagged person is now the new wolf. For Atanarjuat and Atuat to play wolf, of course, suggests a level of intimacy and contact that incensed Uqi, the man to whom Atuat had been "promised." He saw the game as a threat to his manhood, his social standing, and his command of his own future.

Adults and children played a wide range of additional games as well, and of course engaging in simple activities was a popular way to kill time. (When I was with an Inuit family on a three-day whale-hunting trip, we spent an entire afternoon trying to knock a bone off a boulder by throwing small stones at it.) And even though winter fills more than two-thirds of each year, children also enjoyed — and still enjoy — sledding, making snowmen, and building snow forts.

Marriage

Marriage is another central theme in *The Fast Runner*. Atuat wants to marry Atanarjuat, but she has been promised to Uqi since childhood. Marriage in traditional Inuit life was not a formal status, however. When two people found themselves attracted to each other, they would simply move in together to share the same tent or igloo. There was no formal ceremony or any other significant declaration of the new situation; people would simply notice that the two of them were now together.

A man had to think carefully about his ability to provide food before taking a wife. Because the husband was typically considered the hunter, while the wife stayed home to make clothing, mend boots, prepare food, and keep the household together, a young man had to ask himself whether he was prepared to hunt for himself and his wife, instead of living at home and eating the food brought in by his father, brothers, and himself. If he moved out and took a wife, and then was unable to feed her properly or provide enough skins for good clothing, she might eventually have to move back in with her family — a significant loss of face to the young man. Taking a wife, then, meant taking on responsibility, and it also represented confidence in one's hunting skills. A truly skilled hunter might take more than one wife, but only if he was sure he could feed and clothe both of them well. Multiple wives were not uncommon in traditional Inuit life, depending on the ratio of men to women in a community, the availability of food, and the husband's hunting skills. Having two wives who were fat and happy was a status symbol; it meant that the husband was an exceptional hunter.

In *The Fast Runner*, Atanarjuat is an outstanding hunter, so he is able to provide for two wives, Atuat and Puja. He marries Atuat because they are in love, and together they have a son, Kumaglak. But Puja becomes his wife because he needs a woman to help him while he is hunting; someone has to stay at the hunting camp and tend to his clothes and food. Atuat is pregnant, so she can't go. Puja weasels her way in, then seduces Atanarjuat while they are away from home. When he returns, she is simply a new part of the family.

Laws and Leadership

In general, Inuit life, while governed by an elaborate and difficult set of taboos, had few outright "laws." Disputes and conflicts were brought to the elders, who would decide how to resolve the situation to the satisfaction of both parties and with an eye toward the overall health of the community.

A key moment in *The Fast Runner* comes when Uqi, frustrated to the breaking point, threatens to kill Aamarjuaq, Atanarjuat's brother. He makes the threat out loud and in public: "Are you making fun of me? If you think . . . ! If you think you're a better man than me, I . . . ! I could . . . kill you!" The script makes the situation clear: because Uqi has uttered a public threat against Aamarjuaq's life, Aamarjuaq is not obligated to wait until Uqi attacks. Aamarjuaq can kill Uqi at any time, and the act will be considered self-defense.

That blurted threat is an essential part of the film because when Uqi utters it, he puts himself in mortal danger. He now has an enemy in camp who can kill him with impunity. So Uqi cannot wait forever before making his next move; if he is going to attack Aamarjuaq, he needs to do it soon. If he waits, he could find himself on the wrong end of the attack.

In most Inuit communities, it was the judgment of the elders that determined guilt and innocence, punishment or reward. The elders were the repository of wisdom for the community; they had lived the longest, survived the greatest number of challenges, and learned the most from the elders before them. One of Zacharias Kunuk's greatest frustrations is that the political system currently at work in the Arctic undermines the traditional system of leadership by the elders. Today, people in their thirties and forties are elected to office, which gives them political power over people twice their age. Under the current system, it is political savvy, not ancient wisdom, that dictates who will lead. During lulls in the filming of *The Fast Runner*, Kunuk was also working on a video titled *Nipi* (Voices). *Nipi* explores his concern that the new political system is out of place in the Arctic. Just as the presence of evil thwarted the proper governance of the elders in Atanarjuat's camp, he feels the presence of a southern political system is thwarting the proper governance of elders in Igloolik today.

Architecture

The architecture in *The Fast Runner* consists of igloos, sod houses, and skin tents, which were used at different times of year and under different circumstances. (Technically, *igloo* simply means "house," despite its current link to a snow or ice dome.) Architecture has changed profoundly since Atanarjuat's time, although most of the change has taken place within the last few decades or so. Today, most families in the Arctic live in suburban-style clapboard houses with furnaces, indoor plumbing, electricity, and TV. The house I occupied in Igloolik differed in only a small number of ways from a typical house in a modern suburb of, say, Detroit. One of the differences was the water and sewer system. Because underground water and sewer pipes would become clogged when their contents froze, and because digging in the permafrost and tundra is both difficult and ecologically disruptive, water is delivered to homes in most Arctic communities by truck. In Igloolik, the water comes from a deep pond just outside the community; the pond is deep enough to still have liquid water in the bottom of it year-round. The truck drivers pull their rigs up to a permanent system of pipes and hoses and fill their tanks directly from the pond. Some effort is made to sterilize the water, but fresh water in the Arctic is relatively pure. (Concerns persist, however, about PCBs and other chemicals that are difficult to detect.) The truck then moves on a regular cycle to the homes and businesses in town. Each building has a large plastic water tank in a utility room with an outside wall. The tank has a pipe that extends through the wall. The driver fastens his truck's hose, similar to a fire hose, to the pipe and pumps water into the tank until it is full. With water in the tank, the household's plumbing functions just as it does in the South, with faucets and flush toilets and showers.

Sewage is handled in the same way, but in reverse. The truck makes its rounds regularly, pumping sewage out of holding tanks generally located beneath each building. (Most buildings in the Arctic are built on posts, with either open air or a "suspended basement" beneath them. This is done to provide a layer of cold air between the building and the ground. Without that insulating airspace, the warmth from the home would melt the permafrost and cause the building to sink into the ground.) In Igloolik, the sewage is hauled to a large open pit on the side of town opposite the water pond. The driver lowers a large hose down from his truck and drains his tank into the pit.

The other common difference I saw between homes in Igloolik and homes in the South involved food. Many Inuit families rely on government subsidy checks for their cash, which they use to buy rifles and ammunition, fishing gear, clothing, food brought in by plane or boat from the South, and other goods. The checks do not provide a fully comfortable living, however, so the food supply is supplemented by hunting. It is not uncommon to see caribou antlers over the outside door of a house and caribou meat frozen solid on the porch. Inside, a visitor might see a freshly caught seal lying on a piece of cardboard on the floor with its belly slit open; family members and guests eat from it whenever they are hungry.

The differences between the architecture of Atanarjuat's time and the houses and buildings in today's Igloolik underscore a significant point that Kunuk and the other Isuma producers want to make. The houses of the "traditional" times, they feel, reflected a brilliant use of local, available materials — snow, ice, hides, bones, driftwood, sod, moss, sinew — in the construction of structures that not only provided shelter from the elements and the animals but also created focal spaces for family interactions, relationships, and social communion. But those structures are important today only in certain circumstances. (Kunuk has grown deeply weary of people asking him whether Inuit still live in igloos.) Today, igloos (in the common meaning of a dome-shaped structure of ice or snow) are used almost entirely for show, as a way to demonstrate traditional skills; for temporary lodging while out on the land hunting; or for gatherings of community members to celebrate important events. During my time in Igloolik, a friend built an igloo behind her house just for fun and a chance to enjoy participating in a cultural event, and a large ice igloo was built next to the schools in preparation for the Return of the Sun festival in January. (The festival celebrates the moment when the sun first peeks over the southern horizon, bringing an end to seven weeks of darkness. The large igloo was made of ice because it is stronger and more durable than snow—but unlike snow, ice is a poor insulator. The temperature inside the ice igloo was well below freezing, but the air in the upper part of a snow dome can reach fifty degrees Fahrenheit.)

In Atanarjuat's time, igloos were a much more common way of providing winter shelter for families. To make one, experienced elders search for snow of the right depth and consistency, and then the younger men cut large blocks and build the igloo under the direction of the elders. Two basic styles of igloo building can be found in the Arctic. One involves cutting the snow blocks and carrying them to a nearby site to build the igloo. The other involves cutting the blocks from the place that will be the interior of the igloo; the men cut and remove the blocks, and the floor of the igloo descends while the walls rise.

Igloo construction requires an intimate knowledge of snow, wind, gravity, and friction. The builder places a circle of snow blocks to form a diameter that suits his needs. Then he uses a snow knife, which resembles a machete, and cuts the tops of the blocks at a sloping angle to begin the upward spiral. Each new block is carefully shaped to fit on the blocks below and to overlap the previous block with an angled edge. As blocks are added to the growing structure, they are positioned to tilt slightly inward, with the overlaps and friction keeping the blocks in place. The blocks form an increasingly small circle overhead, until finally a key block is placed at the top to hold it all together. A hole is cut near the top to allow smoke to escape, and any gaps between the blocks are chinked with snow. A properly constructed igloo will support the weight of a person walking on it.

The interior follows a standard layout. The doorway is given an extended arch, to block the wind and prevent warm air from escaping. The entry is often designed to dip down and then up into the igloo, providing a "well" in which the heavy, colder air can collect. Sometimes the entry arch is made large enough for the storage of equipment and food.

Opposite the entryway is a platform, made of snow and covered with caribou hides, that runs the entire width of the igloo. That platform provides a place to sit and sleep. The people living in that igloo will share the sleeping platform, typically sleeping naked beneath layers of warm caribou hides. Just such a situation leads to Puja's seduction of Aamarjuaq in the movie.

The typical sleeping arrangements, which are echoed in tents and sod houses, also reveal the significance of the stockings that Puja places on the outside of Atanarjuat's tent. Because the brothers could have been sleeping anywhere on the platform that spans the back of the tent, the attackers needed to know the precise position of their victims in order to make the first thrusts of the spears fatal. The stockings ware intended to show Uqi and his thugs where Atanarjuat and Aamarjuaq were sleeping.

On one side of the entryway, a tripod or shelf is set up to hold the *qulliq*, a stone lamp in the shape of a hollowed-out half moon. The dominant woman of the household, usually the main hunter's wife, tends the lamp, filling it with seal blubber that has been pounded to a soft consistency. Along the straight edge of the lamp, she positions delicate tufts of Arctic cotton, a wispy material much like the cotton found in the South. When the blubber is warmed, it wets the cotton, which then can burn with a bright flame. The flame in turn heats more blubber, providing a steady supply of fuel much as a candle does. The woman tending the lamp makes sure there are plenty of burning tufts and a good supply of blubber in the lamp at all times. The qulliq provides the igloo's heating, cooking, and light (in addition to sunlight filtering in through the snow).

The social ramifications of the qulliq are important in Inuit communities. Because the dominant woman tends the qulliq, friction can develop when a man brings a woman home as his wife. Does the mother tend the lamp, or does the new bride? Who will make the statement by trimming the wicks and positioning the seal blubber? How will the other woman respond? These tensions are elevated when a man brings a second wife into the household. Which one will take care of the lamp — and seize the central position by doing so? The resentment that flourishes between Atuat and Puja boils down to these kinds of questions. What role should each woman play? And who should back down when the other asserts dominance?

With a good number of people and a steadily burning qulliq, the interior temperature of an igloo can reach pleasant temperatures. A pot over the qulliq turns meat into soup, and raw meat is passed around for everyone to enjoy. On the floor, a freshly caught seal, hunk of caribou, or frozen Arctic char provides more food for anyone who wants it.

Resources

Part of the allure of *The Fast Runner* involves its glimpse into how people lived in the seemingly inhospitable environment of the Arctic. With winter temperatures that hover around fifty degrees below zero Fahrenheit, strong winds that can blow a person to the ground, seven weeks of darkness without the sun even breaking the horizon (counterbalanced by seven weeks in summer when the sun never sets), and other conditions that seem daunting to southern audiences, the Arctic can appear to offer no hope of survival for human beings, especially in the time before down-filled parkas, GPS units that can lay virtual tracks in a landscape that seems devoid of landmarks, houses made of nailed wood and Fiberglas insulation, and other modern "essentials."

Part of Kunuk's motivation in making videos is to show that Inuit ancestors overcame these obstacles through a combination of genius, creativity, persistence, and patience. A key part of their success lay in the innovative use of local materials, a fact that Kunuk underscores often through the presentation of everyday life in *The Fast Runner*.

One local resource put to good service by the Inuit was driftwood. The Igloolik region has no trees at all; the landscape is a flat expanse of tundra, rock, and ice. But Igloolik, like many parts of the Arctic, receives large quantities of driftwood that comes from places to the south and west, and the Inuit made good use of it when they found it. With the exception of driftwood, Arctic cotton, and a few other bits of useful plant life, however, nearly everything the Inuit ate, wore, or used came from animals.

One of the main sources of food and materials was the caribou. Properly treated, the hides are warmer than any synthetic yet developed. The meat is tender and tasty when raw, although it can get tough when boiled. The antlers are fashioned into tools and weapons, as Atanarjuat demonstrates when he makes his crampons and clubs at the end of the film. And the sinew, called *ivalu*, is good for thread and string.

Caribou were hunted with spears or driven off cliffs. Useful in both approaches was the *inuksuk* (in-UK-shuk; the plural is *inuksuit*, pronounced in-UK-soo-eet). Inuksuit are stone cairns that are often shaped to resemble human beings. They were used for a variety of reasons, including navigation — on top of a ridge, they can be seen for great distances — decoration, and shamanistic rituals.[1] When used for hunting, several inuksuit would be built in two rows that gradually came together at a point. Hunters would scare a herd of caribou and, waving their arms and shouting, drive it between the rows of inuksuit. The caribou would turn away from the inuksuit in fear, perhaps thinking they were people, and gradually funnel closer together as they ran toward the point of convergence. Several other hunters would wait in that area and jump up when the caribou arrived, spearing as many of them as they could.

Seals provide an excellent source of protein and, wonderfully, vitamins. Seal fat is particularly high in vitamin C, which is important; there are few other sources of C in the Arctic diet. Seal meat is also high in fat, which helps in the constant caloric struggle in the North; the meat is so rich, in fact, that eating it can raise your core temperature. Sealskins, which are a beautiful silver or brown in color, are frequently used to make *pualu* (mittens) and vests. The skin of the square-flipper seal makes good rope, and the skin of the bearded seal can be turned inside out, sealed, and inflated to make a buoy useful for hunting sea mammals, such as walrus and whales. (That was Atanarjuat's technique. He would kill a bowhead whale out at sea, attach several sealskin floats to keep the carcass from sinking, and then wait on his rock bench for the whale to wash up on the beach.)

Seals are hunted with harpoons.[2] When the ocean is frozen, seals create breathing holes in several places, giving them access to air. Some of these holes are enlarged to form dome-shaped cavities in the ice; such a cavity, called an *aglu* in Inuktitut, is used for birthing pups and other functions, in addition to breathing. A hunter sneaks up to a breathing hole very quietly — seals can hear a great deal through the ice — and either stands next to the hole or kneels on a fur pad. He waits with his harpoon ready until he senses the tiny vibrations that indicate that a seal is coming up for air. Then he thrusts his harpoon down through the hole. If it strikes a seal, the hunter stands on the rope and digs through the ice to get the animal out. Some hunters use sensors made from slender reeds. The reed is stuck into the hole, and when it wiggles, the hunter knows that a seal is coming up to the hole to breathe.

Uqi kills his father, Sauri, during a seal hunt. Because each hunter stands at one hole and waits, sometimes for hours, for a seal to appear, Sauri is conveniently alone when Uqi approaches him. The seals' sensitive hearing is why Sauri is so annoyed with Uqi for walking up noisily; the hole would be ruined for a long time after that level of noise around it.

Arctic char is another staple in the North. It can be caught in the freshwater streams that snake along the tundra or in the numerous bays along the coast, and it is an exceptionally good-tasting fish. The traditional way to eat char is to let it freeze solid and then slam it against a rock. The fish shatters, and the frozen "fish chips" melt wonderfully in the mouth. Char were traditionally caught with stone weirs. During the migration of the fish along the rivers in salmon-like fashion, Inuit would build a stone dam across the river to keep the char from escaping to the ocean again. Then the fish would be speared and the meat eaten or dried for later use. The creation and attempted use of a stone weir is shown in the Isuma video *Saputi*.

Walruses offer another source of meat, but they can be hard to hunt. On land, they are wary and quick to slip into the ocean. In the water, they are not only difficult to chase and approach but also dangerous; an enraged walrus can topple a small boat and destroy everything in it. Walrus meat has a strong taste that not everyone enjoys, and the meat and hides give off a pungent odor. One of the classic ways to prepare walrus is to butcher the carcass on the beach and remove the hide. The meat is then placed into the hide, which is sewn up into an airtight bundle. The package is then buried beneath a deep layer of rocks on the beach and left there. Typically, walruses are hunted in June and July, which is when the meat is buried. The meat is dug up in December, around Christmastime. Called *igunaq* (EE-goo-nock), this delicacy has the consistency and smell of bleu cheese. In fact, when someone in Igloolik is enjoying igunaq — usually outside, because of the odor — most of the town knows it and comes by for a taste.

Walruses were hunted from kayaks (*kayak* is an English derivation of the Inuktitut word *qajaq*, meaning a small hunting boat). The walrus is harpooned, often several times to counteract the animal's strength and weight, then dragged to shore for butchering.

Polar bears are both a source of food and hides and a rite of passage: a boy was considered a man after he killed his first polar bear. (An Inuit carver named David Ruben Piqtoukun once told me that he calls that rite of passage the "bear mitzvah.") Hunting polar bears made a natural rite of maturity because the animals are so dangerous, both because they attack humans for territorial reasons and because they hunt humans for food when seals are scarce. A saying I heard several times in Igloolik admonished: "If a human and a bear meet, only one will walk away." The danger represented by polar bears is put to use effectively in *The Fast Runner*. The evil shaman Tuurngarjuaq takes the form of a polar bear carcass when Atanarjuat is walking alone near Sioraq. As Atanarjuat approaches, the "bear" springs to life with a hideous growl. Under normal circumstances in the Arctic, stumbling on a polar bear like that would be the last thing a person ever did.

The hide of the polar bear is black and is used for drum heads and other implements. The meat is riddled with *Trichina* worms and must be cooked for several hours before it is eaten; trichinosis is a dangerous affliction for humans—the worms form cysts throughout the body and damage organs, muscles, and nerves. The liver cannot be eaten at all; it contains so much vitamin A, which is seriously toxic to humans.

Polar bears were and still are hunted by groups of men on dogsleds. When a bear is surrounded, the dogs are freed to attack and harass the bear, giving the hunters a chance to get in close enough to throw a spear. Today, polar bears are hunted on a lottery system. The names of all applicants are pooled and a certain number are drawn based on the allotment of licenses given to each community. The recipient of a polar bear tag has twenty-four hours to hunt the bear. If he is unsuccessful at the end of that time, another name is drawn and the tag is given to him. By law, all polar bear hunting must be done with dog teams; no motorized vehicles are allowed. Southern hunters who travel to the Arctic to hunt bears pay fifteen thousand dollars or more for the tag, the transportation by dog team, and the guide services.

Whales offer another supplement to the Inuit diet and income; it was Atanarjuat's skill as a whale hunter that incurred his rivals' jealousy in many of the versions of the legend. Typically, Inuit hunters go after two kinds of whales, beluga and narwhal. These whales are similar in size and shape, with the beluga tending toward white and the narwhal toward gray. The big difference between them is the long tusk that grows out of the narwhal's upper lip. These tusks can reach six feet or more in length, and they are used for carving artistic sculptures. Uncarved, they sell for more than one hundred dollars per foot. Carved well, they can fetch thousands of dollars in the art market.

The whales were hunted by kayak, with harpoons and ropes. Once a whale was securely harpooned, the hunter dragged it back to shore or stabbed it in the water to tire and kill it. Modern whale hunts use open boats with outboard motors. For one whale hunt I participated in, a large number of families converged on a particular bay about three hours by boat from Igloolik. The families camped along the bay while the elders watched the sea. The plan was to wait until a large pod of whales entered the bay and then use the boats to form a line from one peninsula to the other, cutting off the whales' access to the open ocean. Then the boats would work their way slowly toward the narrow tip of the bay, catching the whales as they tried to swim under or around the skein of boats. The plan was not entirely successful, however. Most of the boats reached the shallows without having seen any whales; the whales were able to swim under the boats and escape. But many whales did not leave the bay even after getting past the boats, and quite a few were harpooned and shot. Once a whale was caught, it was dragged to the nearest beach, where several families converged to butcher the carcass. Every family that helped with the butchering got a slab of the blubber, with the greatest share going to the boat that caught the whale. The whale meat, or *krang*, was either gathered for use as dog food or left on the beach; it has a very strong and not terribly pleasant taste.

The Inuit also hunt bowhead whales on a strict schedule arranged through negotiation and court action with the Canadian government and international organizations. As mentioned previously, bowhead whales are among the largest animals on earth, and they were hunted to near-extinction by British, Scottish, and American whalers. Then a ban was put in place to protect the remaining bowhead populations. After a bowhead was caught illegally in Igloolik in 1994—an action documented by the Isuma video *Arvik!*—the courts ruled that the Inuit could hunt one bowhead every two years.

Birds, rabbits, and other small animals fill out the traditional sources of nutrition for the Inuit. They are hunted with spears, snares, rocks, or any other tools at hand. Eggs are collected from nests in season, adding more variety to the Inuit diet. The hunting of birds and the gathering of eggs kept Qulitalik and his family fed and healthy on Sioraq, which is where they were living when Atanarjuat arrived exhausted and bloody.

Clothing

Traditional Inuit clothing showed variations from one region to another, but those variations were largely stylistic. The primary differences were based on gender, season, and personal expression. It is Atanarjuat's distinctive parka design that allows his wife to recognize him from afar when he returns to Igloolik.

The typical outfit for the men consisted of a top, pants, and boots. The cold-weather top was made of caribou and was pulled on over the head. A hood was attached for extra warmth. Patterns and designs on the parka could be made using fur from different parts of the caribou; the fur on the top of the animal's back was typically dark brown or dark gray, while the fur from the belly would be almost white. Seasonal changes also affect the color of the fur, with the caribou's winter coat being much lighter in hue than the summer coat. By working with different parts of the fur taken from animals hunted at various times of year, the creator of the outfit could arrange striking patterns that indicated region, status, or personal preference. Nothing was worn under the parka, because caribou hide is surprisingly warm (and because anything worn under it would become damp and lice-ridden). The "wolf" game uses the bare skin under the parka as a target.

The pants were made of any of several hides — often wolf or bear — depending on the season and the wearer's preference. They functioned like regular pants, usually tying around the waist. Nothing was worn underneath.

The boots could be made of sealskin or some other hide. Sealskin boots, properly made with caribou sinew holding the seams tight, were waterproof. The sinew shrinks when it gets wet, pulling the seams together with enough force to keep water out.

Women's outfits were similar in overall structure. The top, called an *amauti*, was made of caribou had a large hood which was used to carry babies. The baby would sit in the warm hood and hold the woman's hair for support, and the mother could slide the baby around and inside the amauti for nursing. Women in Igloolik today still wear amautis, sometimes traditional ones made of caribou and sometimes southern-style jackets or sweatshirts with large hoods sewn onto them. Some women make their own amautis out of colorful fabric.

Nomadic Life

The small band of families that forms the social landscape in *The Fast Runner* functioned in the typical manner for Arctic communities. Throughout all the hunting and homemaking that filled Inuit lives was the constant need to move, which meant that any given social group could not become so large that it lost its nimbleness. The nomadic camps followed a seasonal cycle to take advantage of caribou migrations and other shifts. Wise elders who had gained experience hunting year after year would know when to move the camp to places where the hunting was likely to be good. Places where caribou had to cross rivers or lakes, for example, made for excellent hunting spots. When the caribou entered the water, they lost many of their advantages, including speed and the use of their hooves as weapons, and hence became relatively easy to kill. Elders would move their camps to follow such rhythms and end up in the right place at the right time. This is why disruptions in the Arctic ecosystem by pipelines, mining, or roads can place serious burdens on Inuit families. The disruptions force the caribou to change their migration patterns, which in turn forces the Inuit hunters to find the herds all over again.

The nomadic cycles also were timed to bring hunters close to polar bear in the fall, when the ocean ice hadn't quite frozen over. The bears gather on the beach and wait for the chance to get out onto the ice in search of seals, and they become relatively easy to find. Similarly, a well-timed nomadic cycle brought the camp to rivers when the char were running, to beaches when the walruses were plentiful, and to the floe edge in time to catch seals.

One of the challenges of a nomadic life was making sure all possessions were highly useful. Traveling Inuit had little tolerance for items that were not directly helpful to hunting or some other aspect of life on the land. As a result, the art that the Inuit created tended to involve the decoration of utilitarian objects such as parkas, harpoon heads, and qulliqs. The widescale creation of art as a market commodity did not occur until the whalers brought with them pots, rifles, and other objects that they were willing to trade for Inuit carvings.

The demands of nomadic cycles also meant that objects needed to be as small as possible. The classic qulliq is about one and a half to two feet in diameter, but one archaeologist on Igloolik found a stone lamp that was just a couple of inches across.

Context

The Fast Runner presents innumerable facets of Inuit culture to audiences, much of it difficult for non-Inuit viewers to grasp. The patterns on Atanarjuat's parka, the wolf game, the contests of endurance and control — these and myriad other elements of Inuit culture flicker across the screen throughout the movie's three-hour length. But however fleeting they might be, these facets are among the tools used by Kunuk and the other Isuma principals to shape and deliver specific, deliberate messages, and Inuit audiences for the most part understand and appreciate the shades and echoes that context brings to those messages.

CHAPTER EIGHT

Local and Global Environments

As Zacharias Kunuk was enduring my endless string of questions throughout my nine-month research project in Igloolik, he made it clear to me that although Isuma was carrying out a visionary program of cultural communication in video, other organizations were pursuing similar paths in different parts of the world. He strongly suggested that I also spend time in the Australian outback, learning what I could about Aboriginal videography.

I took his advice and spent three months in and around Alice Springs, in the heart of the outback, working with Aboriginal video organizations. The situation there is eerily similar to the one I found in the Arctic. One large central organization, the Central Australian Aboriginal Media Association (CAAMA, pronounced "comma"), functions in the Outback in much the same way that the Inuit Broadcasting Corporation does in the Arctic. Both organizations receive the bulk of their funding from their respective federal governments, and both are dedicated to sharing aspects of their particular cultures with the larger European colonial societies that have engulfed them. CAAMA is working to wean itself from its dependence on funding from Canberra while at the same time overseeing a television network called Imparja and also producing an extensive array of videos, CDs, and other items that share and celebrate Aboriginal culture.

Both the Arctic and the Australian outback also have smaller, independent media organizations that are trying to advance their cultures without becoming so fully beholden to their federal governments. In the outback, one parallel to Isuma is a video organization called the Warlpiri Media Association, located in the small Aboriginal town of Yuendumu. I drove the beautiful but treacherous Tanami Track out to Yuendumu during my stay in Alice Springs and worked for a week with the Warlpiri Media Association, following Kunuk's advice and learning as much as I could about this organization as well. The Warlpiri group produces interesting and sometimes controversial videos on a broad spectrum of subjects; the videos range from an unblinking look at the struggle with alcoholism in Yuendumu (and the domestic violence that goes with it) to humorous depictions of the creativity required to maintain a car in the Outback. And much like Isuma, the WMA sees itself as a subversive organization dedicated to resisting the colonial enterprises around it.

Several scholars have studied and written about Aboriginal video efforts, most notably Faye Ginsburg and the late Eric Michaels. Ginsburg has explored the intersection of media and Aboriginal culture, focusing primarily on the effect the incorporation of non-indigenous media forms has on the society that adopts them. Michaels focused more fully on the audience end, exploring the ways in which Aboriginal audiences use media — particularly television — in ways that are unique to their own social structures and expectations.[1]

Both the Aboriginal media organizations and their Inuit counterparts work to find ways to use the newly affordable and widespread medium of video to record, share, preserve, and advance knowledge about their cultures and languages. And they do their work in an environment that is changing with breathtaking swiftness.

One of the most significant changes to the Arctic in recent years was the formation of the territory of Nunavut. Until 1999, Canada had two territories, the Yukon and the Northwest Territories. The Yukon is a relatively small wedge of land just east of Alaska; it was in this region that gold rush fever brought thousands of would-be miners to the Arctic in the late nineteenth century.

The Northwest Territories occupied the largest parcel of the Canadian Arctic, stretching from the Davis Strait on the east, which separates Canada from Greenland, to the Yukon on the west. In the opposite plane, it began at the northern ends of the provinces and continued northward until the land gave way to the Arctic Ocean.

The Northwest Territories, like Puerto Rico or Guam in the United States, functions as a division of the overall Canadian governmental hierarchy. Given its population patterns and its history of voting trends, its government has been largely white and Southern in composition. Beginning in the 1980s, a group of Inuit leaders began discussions about breaking away from the Northwest Territories and forming a new territory. This new territory would encompass a large region of the Canadian Arctic primarily occupied by the Inuit, and it would therefore be run primarily by Inuit leaders. A coalition of Inuit groups began to coalesce around this new plan.

After fifteen years of negotiations with the Canadian government, the idea of a new territory was agreed upon in principle. One of the many arguments the Inuit used to convince Ottawa to support this plan involved the two-peoples nature of the Canadian federation. Canada, something of an amalgam of English and French communities, has long grappled with a significant bifurcation in its society and culture. Canada has two official languages, for example, and in part it recognizes Quebec as a "distinct society." (In fact, special recognition for the French heritage of Quebec dates back to colonial days. England, concerned that Quebec would support the Thirteen Colonies in what is now known as the American Revolution, granted Quebec special status and acknowledged its French culture and roots.) Pointing to that recognition of a cultural subgroup, the Inuit negotiators put forth the claim that a similar recognition should be granted to the Inuit, who had never engaged the British, the French, or the Canadians in combat. Rather, the Inuit had simply been informed of their Canadian citizenship and had been expected to behave accordingly. The negotiators argued that such an imposition would be legitimate only with Inuit approval, and that such approval would not be forthcoming without some changes.

After further negotiations, on April 1, 1999, the territory of Nunavut was born. (*Nunavut* is Inuktitut for "our land.") Carved from a large portion of the Northwest Territories, Nunavut is larger than Alaska and California combined, encompassing a land mass the size of Western Europe. With about 30,000 inhabitants, however, Nunavut is sparsely populated; if it were a nation, it would be the least densely populated on Earth. Greenland, by comparison, is about the same size and has twice as many people.

The inauguration of Nunavut was punctuated by special ceremonies. Speeches, fireworks, games, and other celebrations ushered in the new territory, and with that fanfare came official proceedings. The new territorial flag was unveiled. Ottawa formally recognized the new Nunavut government. Proclamations were given, declaring Inuktitut the official language of the Nunavut legislature, installing the new premier (similar to a governor in the United States), announcing that the capital would be Iqaluit (a matter already decided by popular vote), and taking other necessary steps.

One of the most interesting moves made by the nascent Nunavut government involved the location of territorial offices. Rather than concentrating all the government offices in the new capital of Iqaluit, Nunavut scattered them among the various communities within its borders. This step was taken for two major reasons. First, traditional Inuit society operated under the authority of a collection of elders, rather than a hierarchy that placed one person at the top as a chief or president. To honor that approach to governance, Nunavut would not have a single governmental seat but rather would spread the centers of power throughout the territory. In addition, the competition to become the capital had been lively. Iqaluit was the frontrunner from the start, primarily because of its population and infrastructure, including a large airport that can receive jets after the ninety-minute flight from Montreal. But other communities submitted bids for the capital designation as well. To appease the communities that lost that competition, the founders of Nunavut decided to place various governmental offices in communities outside Iqaluit as well.[2]

It was during the build-up to Nunavut that *The Fast Runner* was created. The initial plan called for the film to be unveiled at the inauguration ceremonies for the new territory, but funding setbacks pushed back the film's release to a later date.

The creation of Nunavut stands as a material milestone in the rapidly changing context of the Arctic. *The Fast Runner* shows people traveling by dogsled, whereas today, the snowmobile and the all-terrain vehicle are the transportation methods of choice. Another significant change not emphasized in the film involves navigation. In a flat, white, virtually landmark-free part of the world, navigation was a highly refined art. Traveling by boat or dog team in this polar desert requires a keen sense of direction coupled with close attention to information most people might miss. During a whale-hunting trip I joined, for example, the Inuk man at the helm of the boat drove us off in a certain direction for a few hours — and then turned. I could see no change in the landscape, no visual clues, no indicators at all that it was time to change direction. I asked him about it, and he said he knew to turn because the ocean currents had changed, and he could feel the shift in his feet as he stood in the boat. On land, a common navigational practice involves the direction of the prevailing winds. The wind causes ripples in the snow, and the direction of those ripples can tell a traveler which way to go. (Compasses in the North are not very helpful. Not only do iron deposits confuse the needle, but Earth's magnetic pole is almost directly northwest from Igloolik.)

With the advent of GPS systems, however, the art of Arctic navigation is eroding. Older Inuit are concerned that the younger generations will rely entirely on their GPS units and choose not to learn true navigation at all. The danger, of course, comes when the GPS breaks, the unit is lost, or the batteries die in the cold. If a traveler is far away from home and unable to read the signs, the odds of a successful return plummet. Disorientation is extremely easy, and once a traveler becomes confused about location and direction, survival becomes increasingly unlikely. Hypothermia, frostbite, dehydration, and starvation become serious concerns.

When *The Fast Runner* was made, elders were consulted often about how people got around, kept track of their surroundings, and managed to return safely in the days before GPS systems and other devices. The producers learned about long-proven methods of navigation, and the film was created to celebrate the new millennium and the Nunavut era with a long look back at how things were done in the old ways.

Today, global warming is bringing another set of changes to the Arctic. Much of *The Fast Runner* shows life on the snowy plains and frozen oceans of Igloolik. But as the planet warms, the winters shrink, and open water can be found where ice prevailed during the filming of the movie. Business interests are buying entire communities along Canada's northern coast, seeking to profit from the newly opened Northwest Passage. And with commerce come clashes for control: at the time of this writing, the Russian government had just planted a flag on the ocean floor at the North Pole, a not terribly subtle gesture indicating the Russian attitude toward the region.

Throughout all these changes, Kunuk and the other Isuma producers continue to emphasize the wisdom of the elders, the value of cooperation, and the contributions the Inuit can offer to the world. Global warming is not caused by the Inuit, they point out, nor was the overharvesting of the ocean's whales. The Inuit have not organized an army, slashed plant life into submission, or depleted the world's reserves of fossil fuels. Kunuk insists that the planet would benefit from the leadership and knowledge that the Inuit can bring to the table, and his films represent his argument to that effect.

When Atanarjuat deliberately misses his rival's head, smashing his club into the ice instead, he makes a declaration: the feud stops now. With that gesture, he invites the return of order, harmony, and prosperity for all to Igloolik. The message is not intended to be local, nor is it locked in the distant path. Through the experience of watching *The Fast Runner*, Kunuk hopes that viewers will come to an understanding about Inuit ways of thinking that can help humankind correct some of its longstanding mistakes.

Isuma mean "think" in Inuktitut.

ajaja (ah-YAH-yah) — a song, often improvised, and typically accompanied by a drum dance. These songs use "ajaja" as a kind of rhythmic refrain.

ajuraq (ah-YUR-ack) — a lead or crack of open water in the sea ice. These often appear in the same place each year.

amauti (ah-MAU-tee) — the parka worn by Inuit women. The hood was oversized and used to hold infant children, who would sit in the hood and hold on to the mother's hair for stability.

angakkuq (ANG-ga-cook) — a shaman.

Iksivautaujaak or Iksivautaujaq (eeck-see-vow-TAU-zhak) — Igloolik Point, part of the island of Igloolik and a popular hunting ground, especially for walrus. It is the site of Atanarjuat's stone seat, where he waited for the whales he caught to drift to shore.

inuksuk (een-OOK-shuk) — a stone cairn, often built to resemble a human being. These cairns are used for navigation and hunting, as well as for some shamanistic rituals.

Isuma (ee-SOOM-ah) — to think. The verb has implications of deep thought or wisdom.

qaggiq (kag-YUK) — a meeting place, often a large igloo used for gathering, feasting, and celebrating.

NOTES

INTRODUCTION

1. Isuma published the script and a small amount of background information in *Atanarjuat: The Fast Runner* (Igloolik Isuma Productions 2002).

1. THE CONTEXT OF THE CREATION

1. The Inuit are not closely related to other Native North American groups. The American Indians, or First Nations, crossed the Bering Sea land bridge approximately ten thousand years ago and moved southward into what is now southern Canada, the United States, and Mexico. The Inuit came along during another drop in the sea levels that exposed the Bering Sea land bridge about six thousand years later. The Inuit found the North American continent already occupied, and many groups of them continued to move east along the northern coast looking for a good place to settle.

2. For more on the relocation, see Tester and Kulchyski (1994, 1939–63).

3. Sally Berger published a clear and accurate history of northern broadcasting in *Felix* in 1995, and Lorna Roth's excellent book, *Something New in the Air* (2005), covers the topic thoroughly.

2. SEEING THE UNSEEN

1. The recently discovered "tenth planet" — identified before Pluto was demoted — was named Sedna in her honor.

2. In traditional Inuit culture, the concept of an afterlife was unclear. It was believed that the soul lived on after death and that it occupied a place not unlike the ordinary world of humans, but the details were not fully fleshed out.

3. THE PEOPLE AND THE PATH OF ISUMA

1. Frobisher Bay was the name Europeans gave to Iqaluit. The city's name has now reverted to Iqaluit, in keeping with a trend throughout the Arctic of restoring Native place names, but the bay itself retains the name of Frobisher Bay.

2. Henry Glassie, in conversation, August 12, 1997.

3. I emphasize that this approach to authenticity does not mean that New Age wannabes who wear feathers and build sweat lodges in their backyards should be considered authentic Natives. Most of those people adopt iconic images — fringed coats, moccasins, and so forth — without understanding their meaning or history. They might be on spiritual journeys, struggling to find meaning in an absurd universe and a misguided society, but they rarely immerse themselves so fully as to adopt and embrace the culture they are "trying on." The point here is that while Cohn will never be as Inuit as Kunuk is, his presence on the Isuma team does not diminish claims that Isuma's videos are representative of Inuit culture.

4. ISUMA'S MOTIVES

1. There are complex reasons for changing the q to an r, but they boil down to pronunciation. In Inuktitut, a q represents a sound that is like a k and an r put together. In fact, in the syllabic form of writing, the symbol for q is a merger of the symbols for k and r. So when the -ga is added to a word, basically the g and the k part of the q sound are dropped.

5. THE LEGEND AND ITS VARIANTS

1. The ellipses are in the script and represent pauses, not elided words.

2. Rasmussen himself is a key character in Isuma's second major film, *The Journals of Knud Rasmussen*. The film explores the first encounters between the Inuit of the Igloolik region and explorers from outside.

3. Folklorists have found that details such as names are often fungible in oral literature. The underlying roles and relationships are often more significant.

6. REVIEWS AND AWARDS

No notes.

7. LIFEWAYS AS CONTEXT

1. For an excellent book about inuksuit, see Hallendy (2000).

2. Harpoons are different from spears. A spear is a shaft with a fixed point and is thrust or thrown. A harpoon also has a long shaft, but the point, which has a rope tied to it, is designed to come off. When the harpoon is driven into an animal, the shaft falls free, but the point remains embedded in the flesh. The rope coming from the point is tied to a float, in the case of marine mammals, which both tires the animal and keeps the carcass from sinking. In modern hunting the harpoon is thrown first, attaching the float to the animal, and then the animal is shot with a rifle. That way the carcass is not lost when the animal dies.

8. LOCAL AND GLOBAL ENVIRONMENTS

1. See, for example, Ginsburg (1993, 1995) and Michaels (1994).

2. In addition to voting on the site of the capital, people in the region were asked to vote on an important attribute of their upcoming government. A referendum proposed that the Nunavut legislature be the first in the world to mandate fifty percent participation by women. To make this work, every district would have an even number of representatives. The ballot would be divided by sex; the top men would take half the positions and the top women the other half. The proposal was defeated in the referendum, however.

BIBLIOGRAPHY

Anderson, Jason. 2002. "Atanarjuat: The Fast Runner." *Eye Weekly*, April 11. http://www.eyeweekly.com/archived/article/39956. Last accessed April 25, 2009.

Andrews, Nigel. 2001. "Ullman's Barmy Army." *Financial Times of London*, May 23. http://specials.ft.com/timeoff/film/FT3113653NC.html. Last accessed April 26, 2009.

Angilirq, Paul Apak, Zacharias Kunuk, Hervé Paniaq, and Pauloosie Qulitalik, eds. 2002. *Atanarjuat: The Fast Runner*. Toronto: Coach House Books and Igloolik NU: Isuma Publishing.

Atwood, Margaret. 2002. "Atanarjuat: The Fast Runner." *Globe and Mail*, April 10, R10.

Bauman, Richard. 1986. *Story Performance, and Event: Contextual Studies in Oral Narrative*. Cambridge: Cambridge University Press.

Berger, Sally. 1995. "Time Travelers." *Felix* 2, no. 1: 102–12.

Dawson, Tom. 2002. "Atanarjuat—The Fast Runner." British Broadcasting Corporation. http://www.bbc.co.uk/films/2002/01/22/atanarjuat_review_2002 _review.shtml. Last accessed April 25, 2009.

Dujsik, Mark. 2002. "Atanarjuat (The Fast Runner)." Web site: Mark Reviews Movies. http://mark-reviews-movies.tripod.com/reviews/A/atanarjuat .htm. Last accessed April 25, 2009.

Ebert, Roger. 2002. "The Fast Runner." *Chicago Sun-Times*, June 28. http://roger ebert.suntimes.com/apps/pbcs.dll/article?AID=/20020628/REVIEWS/ 206280303/1023. Last Accessed April 26, 2009.

Evans, Michael Robert. 2008. *Isuma: Inuit Video Art*. Montreal: McGill-Queen's University Press.

———. 2000. "Sometimes in Anger: The Struggles of Inuit Video." FUSE 22, no. 4: 13–17.

Fleming, Kathleen. 1996. "Igloolik Video: An Organic Response from a Culturally Sound Community." *Inuit Art Quarterly* 11, no. 1 (Spring): 26–34.

Ginsburg, Faye. 1995. "Mediating Culture: Indigenous Media, Ethnographic Film, and the Production of Identity." In *Fields of Vision: Essays in Film Studies, Visual Anthropology, and Photography*, 256–91. Berkeley: University of California Press.

———. 1993. "Aboriginal Media and the Australian Imaginary." Public Culture 5:557–78.

Groen, Rick. 2002. The Sublime North." *Globe and Mail*, April 12. http://www .theglobeandmail.com/servlet/ArticleNews/movie/MOVIEREVIEWS/200 20412/RVATAN. Last accessed April 26, 2009.

Gunderson, Sonia. 2004. "Zacharias Kunuk: Running Fast to Preserve Inuit Culture." *Inuit Art Quarterly* 19, no. 3/4 (Winter): 48–52.

Hallendy, Norman. 2000. *Inuksuit: Silent Messengers of the Arctic*. Washington DC: Douglas and McIntyre.

Hoberman, Jim. 2002. "Lux et Veritas." *Village Voice*, March 19. http://www .villagevoice.com/2002-03-19/film/lux-et-veritas/1. Last accessed April 19, 2009.

Howe, Desson. 2002. "Fascinating 'Atanarjuat': Lessons of the Thaw." *Washington Post*, June 21, WE44.

Igloolik Isuma Productions. 2002. *Atanarjuat: The Fast Runner*. Toronto: Coach House Books and Igloolik NU: Isuma Publishing.

Johnson, Brian D. 2001. "Arctique Magique." *McLean's*, May 28, 48.

Kupaaq, Michel. 1991. Interview conducted as part of oral-history project organized by Inuit elders in cooperation with the Igloolik Research Centre, Igloolik NU. Interviewed by Louis Tapardjuk. Translated from Inuktitut to English by Louis Tapardjuk. Tape no. IE195. July 24. Used with permission.

———. 1990. "Atanarjuat." The story was gathered as part of an oral-history project conducted by the elders' association in conjunction with the Igloolik Research Centre, Igloolik NU. Interviewed by Therese Ukaliannuk. Translated from Inuktitut to English by Louis Tapardjuk. Tape no. IE128. March 6. Used with permission.

Lacey, Liam. "Atanarjuat: The Fast Runner." *Globe and Mail*, November 30, 2002. http://www.theglobeandmail.com/servlet/Page/document/v5/con tent/subscriber?user_URL=http://www.theglobeandmail.com%2Fservlet %2Fstory%2FLAC.20021130.RVXRIT30-7%2FTPStory%2F%3Fquery%3D Atanarjuat&ord=47488572&brand=theglobeandmail&force_login=true. Last accessed April 26, 2009.

Lord, Albert. 1971. *The Singer of Tales*. New York: Atheneum.

Marks, Laura U. 1998. "Inuit Auteurs and Arctic Airwaves: Questions of Southern Reception." *Fuse* 21, no. 4: 13–17.

Michaels, Eric. 1994. *Bad Aboriginal Art: Tradition, Media, and Technological Horizons*. Minneapolis: University of Minnesota Press.

Monk, Katherine. 2001. "Native Film a Festival Revelation." *Vancouver Sun*, September 28, F7.

Nesselson, Lisa. 2001. "Atanarjuat the Fast Runner." *Variety*, May 18–19.

Onstad, Katrina. 2001. "Small Scale Story of Epic Proportions." *The National Post*, September 11.

Paniaq, Hervé. 1990. Interview conducted as part of oral-history project organized by Inuit elders in cooperation with the Igloolik Research Centre. Igloolik NU. Interviewed by Louis Tapardjuk. Translated from Inuktitut to English by Louis Tapardjuk. Tape no. IE141. March 24. Used with permission.

Panippakuttuk, Zachariasie. 1991. Interview conducted as part of oral-history project organized by Inuit elders in cooperation with the Igloolik Research Centre, Igloolik NU. Interviewed by Louis Tapardjuk and George Qalaut. Translated from Inuktitut into English by Louis Tapardjuk. Tape no. IE200. September 24.

Pitseolak, Peter, and Dorothy Eber. 1975. *People from Our Side: An Eskimo Life Story in Words and Photographs.* Bloomington: Indiana University Press.

Pulver, Andrew. 2001. "Atanarjuat: The Fast Runner." *The Guardian,* August 21. http://www.guardian.co.uk/culture/2001/aug/21/artsfeatures.drama. Last accessed April 26, 2009.

Quintin. 2001. "Les fableaux destin d'Amélie Poulain." *Cinéma Scope* 9 (December): 72–73.

Rasmussen, Knud. 1929. *Intellectual Culture of the Iglulik Eskimos: Report of the Fifth Thule Expedition.* Vol. 7, no. 1. Copenhagen: Gyldendalske Boghandel, Nordisk Forlag.

Rea, Steven. 2002. *Philadelphia Inquirer,* June 21.

Roth, Lorna. 2005. *Something New in the Air.* Montreal: McGill-Queen's University Press.

Said, S. F. 2001. "Atanarjuat the Fast Runner." *Daily Telegraph* (London), August 16, 19.

Scott, A. O. 2002. "A Far-Off Inuit World, in a Dozen Shades of White." *New York Times,* March 30. http://movies.nytimes.com/movie/review?res=9D04E7 DC163AF933A05750C0A9646C8B63&pagewanted=print. Last accessed April 25, 2009.

Shubow, Jason. 2003. "Cold Comfort: The Misrepresentation at the Center of *The Fast Runner.*" *American Prospect* (online), February 28. http://www.prospect .org/cs/articles?article=cold_comfort. Last accessed April 24, 2009.

Tester, Frank James, and Peter Kulchyski. 1994. *Tammarniit (Mistakes): Inuit Relocation in the Eastern Arctic 1939–63.* Vancouver: University of British Columbia Press.

Turan, Kenneth. 2002. "The Fast Runner (Atanarjuat)." *Los Angeles Times,* June 14. http://www.calendarlive.com/movies/reviews/cl-movie000041639jun 14,0,6376492.story. Last accessed April 25, 2009.

Wachowich, Nancy. 2002. "Interview with Paul Apak Angilirq." In Angilirq et al., *Atanarjuat: The Fast Runner.* Toronto: Coach House Books and Igloolik NU: Isuma Publishing.

White, Jerry. 2001. "Northern Exposure: Zacharias Kunuk on Atanarjuat (*The Fast Runner*)." *Cinemascope* 9 (December): 31–33.

Chirac, Jacques, xviii, 100
Christianity: as dominant religion
   in Arctic, 30; Inuit conversion
   to, 5–6, 28, 29, 44; and
   syncretism, 45
Cinéma Scope, 87–88, 96
clothing, 4, 118–19
Cohn, Norman, 6, 8–9, 44, 49;
   biographical information, xvii,
   34–37; and birth of Isuma, 39; on
   changes to Atanarjuat legend in
   Fast Runner, 59; collaboration
   with Kunuk, 33–34; expertise
   in videography, 35–36; filming
   of Fast Runner, 56, 94, 95, 96;
   on "industrial component," 54;
   Isuma business responsibilities
   of, 37, 55; on nondidactic
   methods, 89–90; non-Inuit
   background, 34–35, 129(3n3);
   and screenplay for Fast Runner,
   63, 85; videos: The Journals of
   Knud Rasmussen, 3, 5, 37, 44, 47,
   62, 130(5n2); Two Strangers in
   Frobisher Bay, 33
Cousineau, Marie-Hélène, 15

Dawson, Tom, 93–94
Documenta (Kassel, Germany), 90
dogsleds, 12, 51, 125
Dorset culture, 3
drum dancing, 41, 104
Dujsik, Mark, 96–97

Ebert, Roger, xviii, 99–100
Edinburgh International Film
   Festival, xvii, 87
elders: Isuma's collaboration with,
   39, 43, 49–50, 61, 125–26; requests
   made by, 46; role in Inuit
   society, 61, 107–8, 124

Enuk, 48
Ewerat, 4
Eye Weekly, 89

The Fast Runner: authenticity of, 19,
   52, 99; awards won, xvii–xviii,
   86–87; camera work in, 56, 94–
   95, 96; at Cannes Film Festival,
   xvii, 86, 94–95; consultation
   with elders in making of, 50,
   61, 125–26; critical acclaim
   of, xviii, 87–100; depiction of
   Atanarjuat legend in, 57–59,
   60–61, 63–75; depiction of elders
   in, 49–50; erotic nature of, 95;
   as first feature-length by Inuit
   filmmakers, xvi; funding of,
   55–56; as masterpiece, 99–100;
   mythology in, 31; narrated
   event of, 102; negative critiques
   of, 96–97; number of people
   employed in, 55; pace of, 96–98;
   presents Inuit culture and values
   to world, xvii, 18, 51–52, 57–58,
   91, 92–94, 120, 126; reception of
   by Inuit, 91; script writing, 50,
   63, 78, 85; spiritual forces in,
   19–26; use of amateur actors in,
   36, 86; use of Inuktitut language
   in, 57, 86
Felix, 52, 98–99, 129(1n3)
Festival International du Nouveau
   Cinema et des Nouveaux Medias
   de Montreal, xvii–xviii, 87
Financial Times, 94–95
fishing, 11, 42–43, 115
Flaherty, Robert, 49, 51
Flanders International Film
   Festival, xvii, 87
Fleming, Kathleen, 90
food, 4–5, 109, 113–18

IN THE INDIGENOUS FILMS SERIES

The Fast Runner
Filming the Legend of Atanarjuat
Michael Robert Evans

To order or obtain more information on
these or other University of Nebraska Press
titles, visit www.nebraskapress.unl.edu.